WHILE KEEPING MY DISTANCE

Random Reflections During a Pandemic

Rev. J. Ronald Knott

Sophronismos Press, Louisville, Kentucky

WHILE KEEPING MY DISTANCE
Random Reflections During a Pandemic

Copyright © 2020 by J. Ronald Knott
All rights reserved.

No part of this book may be used or reproduced in any manner whatsoever without permission except in the case of brief quotations embodied in critical articles or reviews.

For information address:
Sophronismos Press
1271 Parkway Gardens Court #106
Louisville, Kentucky 40217

Cover Design & Book Layout: Tim Schoenbachler

ISBN: 978-1-7335457-3-0

Also by J. Ronald Knott

All books published by Sophronismos Press

BOOKS FOR CLERGY

INTENTIONAL PRESBYTERATES
(Spanish and Swahili editions available)

FROM SEMINARIAN TO DIOCESAN PRIEST
(Spanish edition available)

THE SPIRITUAL LEADERSHIP OF A PARISH PRIEST
(Spanish & Vietnamese editions available)

INTENTIONAL PRESBYTERATES: *The Workbook*

A BISHOP AND HIS PRIESTS TOGETHER:
THE CHARACTER OF A PASTOR IN EXERCISING AUTHORITY

PERSONAL GROWTH PLAN: *A Handbook for Priests*

HOMILIES / SPIRITUALITY

AN ENCOURAGING WORD
ONE HEART AT A TIME
SUNDAY NIGHTS
AFFIRMING GOODNESS
THE LORD IS CLOSE TO THE BROKENHEARTED
A PASSION FOR PERSONAL AND VOCATIONAL EXCELLENCE
OUR JOURNEY OF LENT
I JUST HAD TO LAUGH
BETWEEN COURAGE AND COWARDICE

FOR THE RECORD BOOK SERIES

FOR THE RECORD:
Encouraging Words for Ordinary Catholics, Volumes I - XV

FOR THE RECORD ANTHOLOGIES - Vols. I, II, III

For information about eBook and printed editions of Father Knott's books, go to: www.ronknottbooks.com

Table of Contents

Introduction 9
Going To Bed 11
Living Alone 15
Stepping Out of Your Comfort Zone 19
Exploring Your Secrets 23
Paying Attention 27
Wishful Thinking 33
Savor 37
Toilet Paper 41
The Amazing Human Body 43
An Identity Crisis 47
On Embracing "New Realities" 51
Living Alone II 55
Living In a World of Disease and Unease 61
Getting Tired of Extremism 65
Entropy and Senescence 69
In The Stillness 73
When It's Time to Let It Go 77
People Watching 81
Do I Hear a Ringing in My Ears? 85
Home Alone 89
Having a Safe Place to Live 93
Leaving a Legacy 97
Safety Fatigue 101
Trying to Keep No Enemies 105
Standing on Holy Ground 109
Dragging On 115
From Excluded to Included 119
Walking on Thin Ice 123
Golden Years Have Become Stolen Years 125
As the Days Slip Away 129
If It Ain't Messy, It Ain't Real 133
Misplaced Anger 137
Its Really About Arrogance 139
What Does "Normal" Feel Like? 141
The Freedom to Choose Our Attitude 145

Dedication

*To all the "essential workers"
who have risked their lives
to protect and save ours.*

Introduction

This is a series of periodic reflections published on my blog (www.FatherKnott.com) during the early days of the COVID-19 pandemic of 2020. Since there was absolutely nothing I could do about the pandemic itself, I decided to use my time to focus on doing well the "ordinary things" that many people do on a regular basis without much thought and then write about them. In the words of Flannery O'Connor, "I write because I don't know what I think until I read what I say. " By becoming personally more intentional about doing those "ordinary things" with care and focused attention and writing about them, my hope is to inspire others to maybe do the same even after the pandemic passes.

Going to Bed

Most people "go to bed." It is something that most of us do every night, but it occurred to me that most of us probably do it without much thought or real intention.

During this pandemic, on my 76th birthday in fact, I decided to make "going to bed" more of a sacred and purposeful ritual beyond merely "hopping into the sack" and rattling off a few prayers "just in case" I don't wake up again!

Living alone, I have gotten into the habit of getting the most mileage I can out of my bed sheets between washings. Since retirement, I haven't even been making my bed as often as I used to because I never know when the desire for a quick nap might overtake me. It is very much akin to the complaint we used to give our mother when she insisted we wash the windows in the spring. "Why bother? They'll just get dirty again."

In my birthday musings I resolved that I would start being more intentional about my nightly "going to bed." I decided to treat it as the sacred ritual it deserves. I came to the conclusion that I would start preparing my bed with care and attention.

First, there is something to be said for fresh clean sheets (or even better, new ones), "turned down" to look like an engraved invitation to enter a sacred place where your body is invited to rest itself. I decided to see my bed as a "sacramental," a holy object for rest and renewal after a wearisome and stressful day.

Second, atmosphere is important. There is something to be said for order, lighting and even aromas. I decided to make sure all my clothes are put away, the lighting is soft and welcoming and even the smells are inviting, especially if I intend to relax for a while with a good book. Things like scented candles and fresh flowers need not be reserved only for the living room and dining room when guests come over.

A relaxing warm shower, with a special soap or body wash, followed by fresh, weather-appropriate nightwear, and a good book (prayer or inspirational) all tell the body that it is time for rest without the need for sleeping pills or alcohol that anesthetize the mind and trick the body. I already knew it is best to avoid watching the news an hour or two before going to bed, especially these days.

I understand that these rituals probably need to be adapted for couples, but I think these rituals can certainly be adapted, and once adapted, they might serve to strengthen their bond by making "going to bed" more restful, relaxing and peaceful. Do it as a surprise for your partner!

If you have any health care workers in your home (or any other persons required to work outside the home), you might consider rewarding them by carrying out these rituals for them! Help them by creating a haven of rest, a place of comfort, a sacred recovery sanctuary they can come home to. Get some flowers, place some small chocolates on the side table, light a candle, turn down the bed, lay out the night clothes, buy the nice body wash, fluff the towels, offer a prayer book, create an atmosphere of quiet - ask them what else they need to rest up before going back out.

I once heard a German wise saying that goes like this: "A clear conscience makes a soft pillow." I am thinking here about "going to bed" free of fear, dread, pain or guilt - fear of being robbed and attacked, dread of what tomorrow will bring, pain that is chronic (either physical and emotional) or guilt about some unresolved injustice. Whoever is free from those demons should especially thank God before going to bed.

Along that same vein, maybe it's time to bring back the ancient practice of "examining our consciences" so that we can take stock of our bad choices, thoughtless judgments and lazy decisions in order to become masters of ourselves and be able to focus our lives in more life-giving directions. If we cannot establish mastery over ourselves, we will eventually become victims of our own passions.

The Roman philosopher Seneca said, "We should every night call ourselves to an account. What infirmity have I mastered today? What passions opposed? What temptation resisted? What virtue acquired? Our vices will abort themselves if they be brought every day to the shrift." Even secular intellectuals have recognized the value of calling oneself to account by using the term "autocritique," a "methodological attempt to step away from oneself through a process of self-objectification."

St. Bernard taught: "As a searching investigator of the integrity of your own conduct, submit your life to a daily examination. Consider carefully what progress you have made or what ground you have lost. Strive to know yourself. Place all your faults before your eyes. Come face to face with yourself."

St. Pius X summed up our long tradition in this regard when he said, "The excellence of this practice and its fruitfulness for Christian virtue are clearly established by the teaching of the great masters of the spiritual life." Leonardo da Vinci was right when he said, "One can have no smaller or greater mastery than mastery of oneself."

Whatever you do, do it well, whether it is eating or sleeping or working. Be more intentional. Savor each moment. There is so much today that we have so little power over, why not take control of the little we can? Other-love begins with self-love. Why not make the ordinary, like going to bed, a sacred life-giving ritual?

Living Alone

In 2019, 35.7 million Americans lived alone. 28% of all US households. That was up from 13% of households in 1960 and 23% in 1980, according to the US Census Bureau. In 2020, probably 30% of all household are made up of individual people living alone.

Of the 30% of the population living alone, there are some who hate it, some who have no choice and some of us who love it and would have it no other way. I love people, but I thrive on living alone. I may live alone, but I am never lonely. I have also come to know that the thing that makes you exceptional can also make you lonely. As one who thrives on living alone, I have some observations to share.

The first observation is that those of us who live alone are often the object of pity. Pity can, of course, be a form of condescension. However, I also know from listening to people who are married that marriage can actually sometimes exacerbate loneliness. I am sure that some, especially those who hate living alone or who simply have no other choice about it, are so miserable that they deserve some pity. I am not one of them. As a diocesan priest (sometimes referred to a "secular priest"), our charism is not living in a religious community, but living alone. True, in days past we may have lived in a house with other priests, but that was more circumstantial than intentional. Some probably even enjoyed it. I have always understood that diocesan priests are the "solitaries" of the clergy world. As a diocesan priest, my worst nightmare is being forced to live in a house full of priests. I have always been able to work with other priests, I am friends with some of them, but I don't want to live with them. At age fifty, I even purchased an "in-home health care policy" to protect myself from having to go to a "priest retirement home." My choice in no way minimizes the value of what other priests have chosen.

Just as some get their energy by being an "us," some of us get our energy from being a "me." Solitude can be unbearable without healthy self-love. Just as some get their energy by being attached to another and suffer when being alone, some of us get our energy by being alone and we do not suffer from the absence of a full-time other. We have learned that solitude, rather than being an affliction, can actually be a wellspring of creativity and imagination.

As a public person, I have always enjoyed being with people, but I have also enjoyed being alone without the need to impress people, bargain with them about things like when and what to eat or not eat, what color car to buy or what color to paint the walls, where to go or not go or have to listen to their odd noises, both voluntary and involuntary.

One of the best things about living alone and being single is the freedom to relate to many people at the same time, without anyone being jealous or suspicious or controlling. The biggest disadvantage of being single in a coupled world is that you are, most of the time, the odd-man out! The most irritating time is when someone has to "pull up a chair" to make room for you at a table of couples. It seems that you inevitably end up being number three, five, seven, nine or eleven - always the "odd" number!

Another of the good things about being single and living alone that I have learned are the possibilities for generosity that solitaries have that partnered people sometimes do not. Solitaries, unrestricted by marriage and family financial obligations, are much freer to share their time, talents and treasure with "the many."

During this pandemic, I have noticed how many times people have talked about the awful prospect of "dying alone." They think the only good way to "go" is having people holding your hands and talking to you. I may regret saying this, but I could probably handle dying alone much better than most people because I have grown used to my own company and being in an ongoing dialogue with my Creator. As I see it, we all die alone anyway. I see no need for a lot of bedside commentary or drama. I want to be able to say my prayers, shut up and slowly "go to sleep." I want to slip away in silence and hopefully without pain. I remember working at Saint Joseph Infirmary during college. When a member of an "Irish Traveller" family (mistakenly called "gypsies") was dying, a huge number of those family members would show up to comfort them as they died. There is much about the "Irish Traveller" culture to be admired, but for me personally, this is not one of them.

If you are partnered and hate it, you have my pity! (I am praying especially for the victims of domestic violence that is skyrocketing during this pandemic. To be forced to live with an emotional and physical terrorist is to experience hell on earth.) If you live alone and hate it, you have my pity. If you are partnered and thrive on it, I am happy for you. If you live alone and thrive on that, I can resonate. Whatever floats your boat! Whichever it is, however, during this pandemic I suggest that you try to be even more intentional about celebrating and enjoying your unique situation as best you can. Saint Francis de Sales said, "Be who you are and be that well!" Saint Paul teaches us, "Whatever you do, work at it with all your heart …" (Colossians 3:23).

STEPPING OUT OF YOUR COMFORT ZONE

*If you want something you never had
you have to do something you've never done.*
Thomas Jefferson

I have learned from experience, ever since I left home at age fourteen of my own free will for minor seminary, that the secret to a full and rich life is to regularly take the risk of stepping out of your comfort zone. I learned that, when you do, your world expands and you get a new perspective on your old world in the process. For some people, doing that is just way too scary. As Thomas Merton said, The biggest biggest temptation in life is to settle for too little."

The opposite of "stepping out of your comfort zone," insuring that you have a very narrow life, is summed up in the words of an elderly woman from Appalachia when she was asked why she had never traveled more than two miles from where she was born and grew up. When asked about it, she answered, "I just don't believe in goin' places!"

All my adult life, I have been very intentional about "stepping out of my comfort zone." As the Dr. Suess child's book says, "Oh, the Places You Will Go!" I have tracked my decisions to step out of my comfort zone and listed some of the rewards that have come to me for doing just that in my autobiographical book, *Between Courage and Cowardice: Choosing to Do Hard Things for Your Own Good*. I have tried to follow the advice of Thoreau who said, "Be the ... Lewis and Clark of your own streams and oceans, explore your own higher latitudes ... be a Columbus to whole new worlds within you, opening new channels, not of trade, but of thought ... it is easier to sail many thousand miles through cold and storm and cannibals ... than it is to explore the private sea; the Atlantic and Pacific Ocean of one's being alone ..."

As I said earlier, I have learned that, when you do step out of your comfort zone, your world expands and you get a new perspective on your old world at the same time. Nothing in my life has shown me that truth like my most recent "stepping out of my comfort zone," volunteering in the Caribbean missions of the poor little country of Saint Vincent and the Grenadines. I am often asked, "Why would a person like you, who could afford nice Caribbean cruises, stay in fine hotels and eat from luscious buffets in your retirement, choose to volunteer your time, give your money and place your self in poverty, heat and potholes?

The secret of stepping out of one's comfort zone is to realize that something new, something very good will ultimately come to you in the process. The worst approach to volunteering in the missions is to go there with a belief that you are the only one who has anything valuable to give and they are the only ones who have anything to learn. Often, its the opposite.

Every trip down there, twelve of them so far, has been a learning experience for me. I went into it for this reason primarily - so that their situation would change me, not for me to change their situation. Seeing the contrasts regularly and so vividly, I have learned how stingy people who have everything can be, while how generous people who have nothing can be! Yes, I am there to help where I can, but I am also there to be helped! So far I have come home wanting less, wasting less, seeing things from a better perspective and being more generous and grateful in general - realizations I would never have come to without my stepping out of my comfort zone.

Because of these experiences, I moved from not even knowing there was a country by the name of Saint Vincent and the Grenadines down in the south Caribbean to constantly wondering how this or that weather pattern, resource shortage or spreading epidemic is affecting the people I have met and gotten to know by name. I have indeed been enriched by my "believin' in goin' places!" As the Bishop down there wrote in a letter to me recently, "You have made many friends in Saint Vincent and the Grenadines in the last five years." I have indeed been enriched by that recent decision - to "step out of my comfort zone."

You don't really have to always change your location to experience life differently. Sometimes all you have to do is change your perspective on what is right in front of you! You can actually "go places" right where you are! As Thoreau, as I quoted above, said, "Be A Columbus to whole new worlds within you!" Start by being more intentional about the little things in your present life.

And, you, how much is fear, laziness and the love of comfort limiting the size of your world and the parameters of your experience? Stand up to your fear, laziness and love of comfort! Step out of your comfort zone! Do something you have never done so you can experience something you have never experienced.

Exploring Your Secrets

Here is a scary exercise that some of you might consider. I have done it and believe me it is scary! What is it? Take a pen and pencil and make of list of your most personal secrets - the kind of person that you know you really are, the things that you have done or still do that you are ashamed of or the things for which you would rather die before having them exposed to the light of day. Do it without self-judgment and self-condemnation. We all have scars, sins, wrongdoings, mistakes, blunders, missed opportunities, bad decisions and improper choices in our histories. Remember, there's only one group of people who do not have personal "secrets," and they are all dead.

Of course, I recommend that you destroy your list as soon as you are finished, lest it fall into the wrong hands. It is meant for your eyes only so that you can have more insight into yourself. Socrates said, "To know thyself is the beginning of wisdom!" Shakespeare said, "This above all - to thine own self be true." Jesus said, "You will know the truth and the truth will set you free."

Believing that you have made mistakes is one thing. Believing you are a mistake is another. Examination of conscience and confession of sins, a basic tradition in the Christian faith, has so often been misunderstood and even ridiculed by our culture. We hear people cynically refer to "Catholic guilt." What they are talking about is "shame," not "guilt." "Guilt" says "I have made a mistake." "Shame" says "I am a mistake." If the Church helps us feel "shame" because of who we are, that is bad! If the Church helps us feel "guilt" because of the evil we do, that is good!

In Scripture, as soon as we were created, we are told that God looked at us and declared us "good," "very good!" That came before the story of the fall of Adam and Eve. God never meant Adam and Eve be ashamed of themselves but to simply recognize the wrong they had done - basically to themselves.

In Scripture, it is clear that we were created "in the image and likeness of God" and therefore should never be ashamed of who we are, but own up to the bad we do to ourselves and others. In Scripture, it seems that God is more concerned about our learning from our sins than keeping count of them. He seems to want us to admit our mistakes, not just so that we will feel bad about making them, but so that we can make progress in overcoming them. Devoid of introspection, ignorant people keep repeating the same mistakes over and over again, either because they want to deny them or seek to blame others for them, instead of owning them. Wise people admit their mistakes easily. They know that progress in overcoming them accelerates when they do.

There is a world of difference in believing you are a good person, capable of sometimes doing bad things and believing you are a bad person, capable of sometimes doing good things.

As you review your secrets, please, please, please remember the difference between shame and guilt! Shame is about who you are! Guilt is about what you have done!

In the end, our biggest sin, no doubt, is to get to that place where we start calling good evil and evil good.

Paying Attention

*The most desired gift of love is not diamonds
or roses or chocolate. It's focused attention.*
Rick Warren

I find it amazing how many times we look at things, but never really see what we are looking it. Take a US dollar bill, for instance. Most of us have looked at them thousands and thousands of times in our lifetimes. However, if you ask most people how many colors of ink are used on the back of a one-dollar bill, they can't tell you. Many guess that there are three, maybe two, but in reality there is only one color of ink on the back of a US one-dollar bill - green. That's why they are sometimes called "greenbacks."

Attention is the key to so many things related to our lives. We have to pay attention to walk across the street. We know our relationships are more satisfying if we actually pay attention to one another. Driving a car requires a lot of attention. Our business affairs require our attention. All of this seems somehow self evident.

Attention is noticing and being with something without trying to change it. It means to be able to look at it "as it is," not as we imagine it "should be." Attention takes the time to fully explore, to discover whatever there is to know about something, to watch as things change by themselves without our trying to 'fix' anything.

Attention is patient and attention is kind. No rush. No burden. No criticism.

Healing an injury requires the practice of paying attention, of being with something fully, of focusing upon it over and over again without pushing it away or trying to change it. It is in paying attention that we will discover the tiny threads of healing and transformation that are developing moment to moment. Losing weight requires attention to the food we eat and the exercise we get. It is attention, not judgement, that will help our brains rewire.

Paying attention is ultimately an act of loving kindness towards ourselves. If we love a child, we pay attention to her/him. We watch this child thrive as we give her/him our attention. We know this works. In this way we are not different from the child. We too will thrive with attention and as adults, we have the capacity to give that attention to ourselves. Is that not what we mean when we say to someone when we leave them, "take care of yourself?"

During this time of pandemic, when my world seems to have shrunken a bit, I am trying to pay more attention to things right in front of me, things I have sometimes in the past failed to notice - failed to pay attention to.

Out of fear that I would get fat and lazy, without even being aware of it, I have been paying close attention to what I am eating. I have for all practical purposes, cut out bread, sugar and other carbohydrates. When I want to watch TV, I give myself permission only if I am on the treadmill while I am watching it. So far, I have maintained the weight I lost, I sleep better and I think my immune system has been strengthened.

I haven't been able to travel, go to restaurants, see people at church and visit people at the coffee shop. To replace all that visual and interactive stimulation, I have started to do things that help me pay closer attention to the small, ordinary things. I have gotten up early several times just to fix a good cup of coffee, go out on the deck and feel the cool air, see the opening buds, watch the gentle rain fall on the pond, hear the birds chirp and the trees bend in the breeze. I don't really care what the weather is like because there is something new to notice whatever it is! I read once that "there is not such thing as bad weather, just inappropriate clothing." I have come to believe that "bad weather" is in the eye of the beholder.

I haven't been able to be around a lot of people for the last eight weeks but I have tried to pay more attention to what people are saying when I do talk to them. Instead of preparing what I will say when they finish talking, I try to encourage them to talk more while I pay more attention to what they say - to the person behind the talker.

I don't get out a lot, but when I do I try to really "see" those who are performing vital services. First I try to realize that many of them cannot afford to be safe "in place" like me. I greet them more. I compliment them more. I even tip them more. Giving attention to the men and women who do menial tasks for us is the least we can do.

Even though I had to cancel trip number 13 to the islands, I have not quit my ministry with them and among them. In fact, I have become even more aware that, even though there are needs here in this country, their needs are even more acute. Charity may "begin" at home, but it doesn't have to "stay" at home.

To live well, to live on purpose rather than being passive and letting anything and everything happen, requires disciplined attention.

To live well is a lot like driving a car – you have to be able to see what is going on behind you, in front of you and all around you, but all at once. You have to learn from your past, plan for your future and be alert to what is happening in your life right now.

Jesus reminds us in the gospel to be "watchful" and "alert," warning us that "we don't know when the Lord will come." It says that he "may come suddenly and find us sleeping," so we need to "watch," "wake up" and "pay attention."

Living well, alert and watchful, is hard work. Our lazy side must be stood up to, over and over again. Our lazy side tells us that we have plenty of time, that we can get around to it someday and that we can cut corners for a little while longer. Our lazy side is our sinful side. The best definition of "sin" I ever heard was that it is at its root giving in to laziness. When we "sin," we choose the "easy way" rather than the "right way." Laziness is the opposite of "staying awake and staying alert."

If you look at it closely, all sin is about laziness. Theft has laziness at its root. It is easier to take what belongs to others than it is to work for what is your own. Theft is a lazy shortcut to getting what we want. Gossip has laziness at its root. It is easier to cut others down to our size than it is to build ourselves up. Gossip is a lazy shortcut to feeling good about ourselves. Pornography has laziness at its root. It is easier to relate to an anonymous printed or projected image than it is to build intimacy with real people. Pornography is a lazy shortcut to feelings of intimacy. Excessive eating and drinking has laziness at its root. It is easier to do the things that feel good to our bodies than it is to do things that are truly good for our bodies. Excessive eating and drinking is a substitute for facing unpleasant feelings. Taking recreational drugs has laziness at its root. It is easier to take a pill or snort a substance that gives us an artificial high than it is to work for the high of a deeply spiritual life in relationship with God and others. "Following the crowd" has laziness at its root. It is easier to gain acceptance by "doing what everybody else is doing" than it is to "do the right thing" and risk rejection. Yes, all "sin" is about choosing the "lazy way," about choosing the "easy way" over the "right way."

St. John Paul II gave us some great advice for daily living when he put it this way: "Remember the past with gratitude. Live in the present with enthusiasm. Look to the future with confidence."

*Would that you would meet us doing right
and being mindful of your ways.*
Isaiah 63:7-9; 64:3-4

Wishful Thinking

Wishful thinking is a belief that something specific that you want to be true is true regardless of proven facts. Optimism, on the other hand, is positive thinking based in reality, that something good will happen even if that good is not exactly the good you had envisioned.

During this pandemic, trying to kill more time than usual, I have ended up watching too much television. I believe that I am an optimistic person, but two shows in particular, have opened my eyes to how deeply some people can fall into "wishful thinking" and stay there when every red flag in the world has been waving in their faces for years. "90 Day Fiance" and "Catfish: The TV Show" are two specific, but very popular, examples. Both reveal the stubborn gullibility, and eventual heartbreak, of some naive people who become victims of online dating and relationship scammers. Even after years of being lied to and being let down, years of sending money, the obvious truth escapes them as they cling to the myth supported by their need for something to be true that isn't really true. It is both amazing and sad to watch. The popularity of those shows, along with other voyeuristic day time TV shows like "Maury Povich" and "Jerry Springer," must all come from the same place that old sin of "morose delectation" comes from - taking delight in others people's failures, sins and disasters! There is something about us that simply cannot resist slowing down to look at the car wreck on the side of the road - the bigger the disaster, the more compelling the need to look.

The concept of "willful blindness" comes from the law and originates from legislation passed in the 19th century — it's the somewhat counter-intuitive idea that you're responsible "if you could have known, and should have known, something that instead you strove not to see." What's most uneasy-making about the concept is the implication that it doesn't matter whether the avoidance of truth is conscious. This basic mechanism of keeping ourselves in the dark plays out in just about every aspect of life, but there are things we can do — as individuals, organizations, and nations — to lift our blinders before we walk into perilous situations that later produce the inevitable exclamation, "How could I have been so blind?"

Whether individual or collective, willful blindness doesn't have a single driver, but many. It is a human phenomenon to which we all succumb in matters little and large. We can't notice and know everything. The cognitive limits of our brain simply won't let us. That means we have to filter or edit what we take in. So what we choose to let through and to leave out is crucial. We mostly admit the information that makes us feel great about ourselves, while conveniently filtering whatever unsettles our fragile egos and most vital beliefs. It's a truism that love is blind; what's less obvious is just how much evidence it can ignore. Many of the people on "90 Day Fiance" prove it each and every week! They see only what promotes their "wishful thinking" until the disaster is so obvious they cannot escape.

We make ourselves powerless when we choose not to know. The very fact that willful blindness is willed, that it is a product of a rich mix of experience, knowledge, thinking, neurons, and neuroses, is what gives us the capacity to change it. Like King Lear, we can learn to see better, not just because our brain changes but because we do. As all wisdom does, seeing starts with simple questions: what could I know, should I know, that I don't know? Just what am I missing here?

People who tell us what we want to hear are not necessarily our friends! People who tell us what we do not want to hear are not necessarily our enemies! Prophets are not, as many assume, people who predict the future. They are most often the people who make us look at what's right in front of us! They rub our noses in the truth. That's why they are often killed - not for their lies, but for their honesty. A true friend is one who risks telling us the truth and forcing us to open our eyes to see what we don't want to see. There is none so blind as one who simply refuses to see!

In the end, all of us in some area of our lives refuse to love the truth, but instead try to make true what we love. We are all capable of wishful thinking. What can save us from us are the honest people we invite into our lives - the people who can rub our noses in reality and slap us awake before it is too late!

Savor

When you "savor" something, you enjoy it so much that you want to make it last forever. With that in mind, "savor" carries a connotation of doing something slowly. If you "savor" that chocolate tart, then you eat it slowly, bit by bit, deliberately picking every last crumb off the plate. The word is often applied to eating, but you can "savor" any pleasurable experience, including things like winning a raffle or your moment in the spotlight.

Try savoring everything you do, every experience! There is no moment that cannot be savored — even those routine moments, even those times when you're alone with nothing to do.

Savoring is about learning to live presently, to fully enjoy the gift of each moment, to give that moment the space and attention it deserves. It takes practice, but it's a "delicious" practice.

As I have mentioned before, one of the things I like to do, especially when the weather is balmy or there is a gentle rain falling, is to get up early, right after the sun comes up, and go out on the deck with a cup of really good coffee and just sit there in the quiet and let the smells, breezes, bird chirping and rain falling on the pond in front of me wash over me. Talk about "savoring" the moment! I don't even like to get up early, but those "savoring" moments make it all worthwhile.

Savoring, a magical act, is usually applied to eating good food. Take a single square of dark chocolate and put it in your mouth, but don't chew and swallow it. Let it sit there, as you savor it, noticing its earthy notes, hints of citrus, the richness of its texture as it melts in your mouth. You swallow it almost regretfully after letting it linger, fully appreciating the deliciousness of it, giving pause to think about the people who grew the beans, who roasted and ground them and hand-crafted them into this square of joy. One of the things I recommend during this pandemic that you use this extra time to savor food by "dining" instead of just "eating."

DINING

One of the problems that causes many people to be overweight is that they eat too much. A big reason people eat too much is that they eat large amounts of food, quickly. It's tasty, so they eat it fast and then get some more!

During the pandemic, I've been trying to avoid eating in front of the TV and embrace sitting down to a "set" table and savoring my food. When I do this, I don't just cram it down my throat, but I pause for each bite and I give it space. I savor it.

This means that I make it possible to really notice every taste of each bite, the texture of it, and give thought to where it came from, who made it, what went into it, and what it will do for my body.

It's hard to overeat when you savor each bite, and take your time. In this way, you can also learn to enjoy healthier foods. You can also eat healthfully most of the time, and then enjoy a bit of birthday cake without overdoing it, because you just need a little bit in order to savor it.

When you savor things, you slow down. You pay close attention — the closer the attention, the more you'll get out of the savoring. You won't rush to the next thing, but stop and give some space to the activity. You won't be worried about what you have to do later, because you are fully enjoying the present.

This is savoring, and it takes practice. You can do it right now, wherever you are: pause and look around you and savor this very moment. Even if it doesn't seem to be special, because let's face it you've done what you're doing a thousand times, savor it anyway. Fully appreciate the gift you've been given.

This is a practice you can do several times a day — find a few rituals for savoring, like enjoying your morning coffee, or taking a bath, or reading to your child, or having a tea ritual in the mid-afternoon. The more you practice, the better you'll get.

Savor everything you do, every experience. There is no moment that cannot be savored — even those routine moments, even those times when you're alone with nothing to do.

Savoring is about learning to live presently, to fully enjoy the gift of each moment, to give that moment the space and attention it deserves. It takes practice, but it's a delicious practice.

> *As you walk and eat and travel, be where you are.*
> *Otherwise you will miss most of your life.*
> Buddha

Toilet Paper

All of us use toilet paper, and unless we have a "problem," we don't think about it too much until somebody yells "shortage," like they have done during this pandemic. Then it becomes, overnight, more valuable than gold to masses of people. The hysteria around the accumulation of toilet paper has been pitiful to watch. It has truly been strange. In reaction to COVID-19, people are going crazy over hoarding, of all things, toilet paper!

Just when you think it can't get any stranger, I came across this related video while I was researching this blog post. There are people who are actually addicted to eating toilet paper! If you don't believe me, go to YouTube and search: *My Strange Addiction - Kesha Eats Toilet Paper.*

If you have a stockpile of toilet paper, I suggest that you sell it while prices are high! Suppliers predict that the market has been so flooded that prices are bound to drop drastically in the near future and people's precious "goldmines" will be pretty much worthless. The only good thing is, if the mice don't get into it, it has no expiration date. It will merely continue to take up valuable space for years to come. You will probably get so tired of working around it, that you will be ready to give it away to a homeless shelter, burn it in the fireplace or just take it to the dumpster.

If we can learn anything from this "toilet paper hysteria," surely it must be this! Resist a "herd mentality" and "following the crowd" and **think** for yourself!

If you have been stockpiling toilet paper on one hand and refusing to wear a mask at public gatherings on the other, you have earned the right, to put it bluntly, to be labeled a "nut case!"

The Amazing Human Body

Psalm 139: 13-18

For you created my inmost being;
you knit me together in my mother's womb.
I praise you because I am fearfully and
    wonderfully made;
your works are wonderful,
I know that full well.
My frame was not hidden from you
when I was made in the secret place,
when I was woven together in the depths of the earth.
Your eyes saw my unformed body;
all the days ordained for me were written in
    your book
before one of them came to be.
How precious to me are your thoughts, God!
How vast is the sum of them!
Were I to count them,
they would outnumber the grains of sand –
when I awake, I am still with you.

During this time of "social distancing," I have had time to pay attention to things I usually don't even think about. One of the "very ordinary things" that I have become more aware of during this pandemic is my own body.

As I passed my 76th birthday at the end of April, I have become more aware of my heart. It is miraculous to me that an organ that size has been pumping day and night, twenty-four hours a day, non-stop for 76 years! A refrigerator can't do that. A car can't do that.! A computer can't do that. A furnace can't do that. It has kept pumping, without stopping to rest, for seventy-six years! It's absolutely amazing, and I rarely stop to think about it.

With all the talk about the shortage of ventilators (breathing machines) and people having to be be intubated (a tube shoved down their throats to help them breathe), I have become very aware of my lungs. They have been putting oxygen into my blood for more than seventy-six years. They started seconds after coming out of my mother's womb. The only time I ever think about my lungs is when I get a lung X-RAY and the doctor tells me what it looks like. The only time I ever got alarmed about my lungs was when I was hospitalized for a blood clot in my leg. The doctor told me in the emergency room not to move off the table I was on because "if that clot comes loose and goes to your lungs, you're dead!" Like my heart, my set of lungs have been working night and day ever since I was born, while awake and during sleep, without my even noticing it.

I have used this time of "social distancing" to be more acutely aware of what I eat and the exercise that I engage in. I do not want to gain weight by becoming a "couch potato." In the process, I have become more aware of my marvelous digestive system. I am trying to see eating as something I do to nourish my body, not something I do to numb myself during boredom and stress. I have become more aware of what happens to what's left of that food when my body has processed out what it wants to eliminate. I know it sounds weird, but I have become more conscious of our amazing Metropolitan Sewer District, not just my own marvelous digestive system. The fact that it can handle the human waste of 1,278,000 people a day so discretely is not something I have normally thought about! When you really stop to think about it, that whole process borders on miraculous in itself.

This time of "social distancing" has offered me an extended period of reflection and introspection. As amazed as I am with noticing the very ordinary things that many of us take for granted, it is not lost on me that at age seventy-six, I am a bit like a used, but somewhat reliable, car with a bit more mileage left on it. This pandemic has opened me eyes to what could go wrong very quickly health wise, even though I am doing everything I can to do good preventative maintenance.

Over all, this pandemic has opened my eyes. It has caused me to be more aware that, most of the time, I really am "simply amazed and forever grateful." Now I have to keep on reminding myself of the words of Jesus, "Fear is useless. What is needed is trust!"

An Identity Crisis

Recently, I had dinner with a friend who I had not seen for a while. We used to meet regularly - maybe every five or six weeks - but because of the pandemic and "social distancing," it was our first time in ten or twelve weeks.

We don't usually talk about work or sports or entertainment, but oddly enough we talk about our personal growth or lack of it. It's sort of two-person introvert support group.

Since we had not met for a while, I came prepared. To "prime the pump" on the discussion, I asked him two questions about how he was handling the pandemic. I asked him (1) what have you been most scared of personally and (2) what have you been most scared of professionally.

I won't share what his answers were, but I can share mine. (1) I told him that I was most afraid of getting sick myself. (2) I told him that I was most afraid of losing my identity.

FEAR OF GETTING SICK: I try to be careful and follow the CDC guidelines, but I don't obsess about contracting the virus. However, I am very much aware that I am in the high risk age group. While I am pretty healthy for my age, at 76 anything could go wrong, at about anytime, without much notice. Because of all that,

I catch myself wondering how I would handle hospitalization, if it came to that, especially if I had to be put on a respirator. I wonder whether I would even allow it if I were in a state where I could make that decision. I know I would ask some very serious questions.

FEAR OF LOSING MY IDENTITY: More than a fear of getting sick, I have found myself going through a mild "identity crisis." An "identity crisis" is a period of uncertainty and confusion in which a person's sense of identity becomes insecure, typically due to a change in their expected aims or role in society.

Yes, I have been "retired" for five years, but I have stayed busy doing quite a few of the things I love to do. I don't have a position or a title, but I have had "my work" and plenty of it. I was flying here and there, to Canada and around the United States mostly, doing priest retreats, convocations and parish missions. I was volunteering in the Caribbean missions and managing my new Catholic Second Wind Guild that supports it. I was helping out at the Cathedral downtown and the Little Sisters of the Poor nursing home down the street. Things were going so well.

Because of this damnable pandemic, all that has basically come to a screeching halt! Maybe some of it will come back, but about the only thing left right now is this blog and a couple of graveside funerals, for which I am very grateful! I cannot fly to other dioceses to do presentations to priests. I can't fly down to Saint Vincent and the Grenadines, taking volunteers with me, to meet with the people I have gotten to know and to work on our projects. I am not allowed to go into nursing homes. Masses at the Cathedral were cancelled. Even now, with a reduced schedule, I am not all that needed for a while.

I wake up these days feeling very aware that I have entered a period of uncertainty and confusion in which my sense of identity has become insecure, due to these unwanted changes in my planned schedules and the scaling down of my role in the church. I keep remembering what one of my nieces said to me the day after her husband died. "I knew who I was yesterday. Today, I don't know who I am!" These days, I am a workaholic with little to do. I am a priest without a ministry. Maybe this is what happens to parents when they experience the "empty nest" syndrome?

I know I like to be in control of things, especially those things that affect me directly. I like to be responsible for my own happiness and do those things that bring me, and those around me, happiness. I like the freedom to choose what I do, when I do it and where I want to do it. I have worked very hard to get to this point in my life. Lately, I feel that I am slowly losing the identity I have worked so hard to build because so much is now out of my control.

Maybe that's what's really bothering me. Maybe this pandemic is exposing the truth that there are more and more things not in my control. Maybe what I am learning during all this is how to "let go" of situations that I can't control and how to live constructively without that control. I have learned from the many seniors that I have known and loved over the years that "letting go" is a huge part of aging.

In the first part of our lives, it was all about learning how to take control of the situations we found ourselves in. Maybe the last part of our lives is about learning to let go of control of the situations we find ourselves in? So far, I don't like it, but maybe I can learn? Maybe I will have to learn.

On Embracing "New Realities"

There's a good chance the coronavirus will never go away completely. Even after a vaccine is discovered and deployed, the coronavirus will likely remain for decades to come, circulating among the world's population. Experts call such diseases "endemic" — stubbornly resisting efforts to stamp them out. Think measles, HIV and chickenpox!

With so much else uncertain, the persistence of the novel virus is one of the few things we can count on about the future. That doesn't mean the situation will always be as dire. There are already four endemic coronaviruses that circulate continuously, causing the common cold. And many experts think this virus will become the fifth — its effects growing milder as immunity spreads and our bodies adapt to it over time.

"This virus is here to stay," said Sarah Cobey, an epidemiologist and evolutionary biologist at the University of Chicago. "The question is, how do we live with it safely?" Americans have only started to wrap their heads around the idea, polls show.

One of the hardest things to wrap my head around is that the way I have been living my life has taken another turn and it is up to me whether I give up or get up. I learned a long time ago that you can be pitiful or you can be powerful, but not at the same time.

When I arrived at the Cathedral of the Assumption in 1983 to begin a time of great transition for me personally, not to mention the people I was called to lead. I had been given the task of "revitalizing" a dying congregation before it was too late. It had had a glorious past. The years of 1890 - 1910 were referred to as the "golden age." One of the questions I tried to answer for myself and get the congregation (what was left of it) was this, "Who said you only get one golden age?" I repeated it to myself and to them, over and over again until we believed it. Once we believed it, we ended up seeing it! We experienced a "second golden age."

When I left there after fourteen glorious years, the thing I had to fight most in my own mind was the belief that I only get one "golden age." In the years to follow, by embracing the future with hope and positive energy, rather than wallowing in what was over and done with, I worked toward experiencing a second personal "golden age." I developed a nationally well-known ongoing formation program for priests with a $2,000,000 grant from the Lilly Endowment. Besides running my newly created Institute for Priests and Presbyterates at Saint Meinrad Seminary, I traveled the United States, England, Ireland, Wales, Canada and the Caribbean as a motivational speaker on the subject. I did Parish Missions, served as a university campus minister and published several more books. In those fourteen years, I experienced my second personal "golden age," but I did not want to spend my remaining years boring people with stories about my past ministries.

When I retired, I thanked God for those two personal "golden ages," but I asked for a third "golden age" in my old age. I began implementing what I came to call the "Catholic Second Wind Guild," a retirement program for myself and other clergy and lay professionals who wished to volunteer in the Caribbean missions. After five years, this third "golden age" was materializing quite quickly. Then, boom, came the COVID-19 pandemic, which has thrown a monkey wrench in many parts of my plans. I can't travel to the islands until who knows when! I have been "laid off" from the Cathedral until the pandemic passes. Invitations to speak at big gathering of priests are drying up. No one is scheduling Parish Missions. I can't even celebrate my 50th anniversary of priesthood. I feel like I knew who I was and where I was going four months ago, but now I don't know who I am or where I am going.

Even though I have been able to continue some of my Caribbean ministry and priest lectures by using "social distancing" and the internet, I know in my gut that going forward will not be something I get to decide, but it will be something revealed to me. I know from experience that when I come to an unexpected fork in the road like this one, the game is not necessarily over. It just means that I am facing another "breakdown that will lead to yet another a breakthrough." I know, in my heart of hearts, that if I surrender to God's plan, and not clutch to my own, things will be good. As I said earlier, it will probably not be something I get to decide. Rather, it will be something revealed to me. Therefore, I am trying to wait in joyful hope for God to reveal my fourth "golden age." If it is half as good as the last three, I will be more than satisfied. I will again be "simply amazed and forever grateful!"

Living Alone II

"Getting used to living alone is not the problem, it's giving it up once you do!"
Lady Rosamund, "Downtown Abbey"

If there is any doubt that we're living in the age of the individual, a look at the housing data confirms it. For millennia, people have huddled together, in caves, in mud huts, in cottages and condos. But these days, 1 in every 4 American households is occupied by someone living alone; in Manhattan, the number is nearly 1 in 2.

Eric Klinenberg recently published *Going Solo: The Extraordinary Rise and Surprising Appeal of Living Alone*, which he calls "an incredible social experiment" that reveals "the human species is developing new ways to live."

True, the benefits of living alone are many: freedom to come and go as you please; the space and solitude to recharge in a social media world; complete control over the bed. In the seminary, we slept in single beds. As a priest, I have to have either a king or queen size bed, even though I usually use only one side!

Still, the single-occupant home can be a breeding ground for eccentricities. In a sense, living alone represents "the self let loose." In the absence of what Mr. Klinenberg calls "surveilling eyes," the solo dweller is free to indulge his or her odder habits — what is sometimes referred to as Secret Single Behavior. Feel like standing naked in your kitchen at 2 a.m., eating peanut butter from the jar? Who's to know? Personally, I have the habit of putting on clothes to go downstairs in the middle of the night, just in case I fall down the steps and people find my unclothed body a few weeks later.

A 28 year old schoolteacher calls it living without "social checks and balances." The effects are noticeable, she said: "I've been living alone for six years, and I've gotten quirkier and quirkier."

What emerges over time, for those who live alone, is an at-home self that is markedly different — in ways big and small — from the self they present to the world. We all have private selves, of course, but people who live alone spend a good deal more time exploring them. Personally, I have a two-floor condo. The upstairs, where people come in, is always clean and tidy. The downstairs, where I spend a lot more time, not so much.

I read about one man who said his living-alone indulgences center on his sleep cycle. A 40 year old record producer said he'll go to bed at 2 a.m. one night, and then retire later and later by increments, "until I go to bed when the sun comes up." These days, personally, I often stay up past midnight. I love to write late at night. Even after I go to bed, I sometimes get up and go downstairs to work on the computer about 2:00 am and then go back up around 3:00 am and go right back to sleep – so far without a problem.

A 70 year old woman who writes a blog on aging, timegoesby.net, has lived alone for all but 10 or so years of her adult life. She said she has adopted a classic living-alone habit: "I never, ever close the bathroom door." Leaving it open "is one of those little habits that makes no difference most of the time," she said. But when guests visit her two-bedroom apartment outside Portland, Ore., she added: "I have to make huge mental efforts to remind myself to close the door.

Like many, she also talks to herself — or, rather, to her cat. "I'll try things out on him when I'm writing," she said. "He'll look at me like he's actually listening. I wouldn't discuss what I'm writing with my cat if someone were around." I don't have a cat, but I do ask myself questions, out loud, when no one is around.

Other people say their greatest eccentricities emerge in the kitchen. Eating can be a personal, even self-conscious act, and in the absence of a roommate or partner, unconventional approaches to food emerge.

"I very rarely have what you would call 'meals,'" said Steve Zimmer, a computer programmer in his 40s who lives by himself in a Manhattan loft. Instead of adhering to regular meals or meal times, he said, he makes "six or seven" trips an hour to the refrigerator and subsists largely on cereal. As for me, I cannot go to sleep with knives on the counter in the kitchen. They have to be out of sight so that an intruder cannot find them so easily.

The founder of the Web site quirkyalone.net, is a kind of unofficial spokeswoman and lobbyist for singletons.

She has had roommates in the past but now lives alone. She said that rather than cooking a big meal for one, an unappealing prospect, she fashions dinner out of "discrete objects": "I'm often, like, here's a sweet potato! Let me throw that in the oven with aluminum foil and eat it." Personally, it's not a problem for me to eat a piece of cake followed by a salad and popcorn, if I am still hungry.

One woman noted that the longer she lives alone, the less flexible she becomes — and the less considerate of others' needs. "If I go on vacation with a group of friends, I feel a little overwhelmed," she said. "I've got to share this room with other people? We have to organize showers?" Personally, I would rather stay home than share a room with someone on a vacation – even if it were a free vacation.

A computer programmer said he is also conscious of becoming too set in his ways, especially where sleeping is concerned. "I just do not sleep as well with someone else," he said. "A lot of homes have double master bedrooms. I can really see the value of that." Personally, I cannot imagine sleeping with someone else in the bed with me.! No way!

My "single habits" are many. I clean my house before the cleaning lady comes every couple of months. I cannot go to sleep unless my car keys are next to my bed "in case of an emergency" during the night. I have to turn off the water and check the stove before I leave the house overnight. Before I go to sleep, I have been known to check the front door several times in a row "to be sure I locked it!"

It is aggravating sometimes to have to "do it all" when you live by yourself, but I wouldn't have it any other way.

Living in a World of Disease and Unease

I am getting sick and tired of trying to stay safe! Just when I thought it might be safe to go out and about, I am told every night on the news that the pandemic in Kentucky is spiking upward! If it would help, I would stand out on my deck and scream as loud as I can! The only thing that stops me is the realization that the neighbors might call the police and have me arrested. Then it would become a classic case of "out of the frying pan and into the fire!" Besides, I would hate to see my photo in the Courier Journal under the headlines, "Local priest loses his mind and is arrested for being a noise nuisance."

I have found that when I get into a state of mind like that, it is at least a temporary relief to think of others who are in a worse state than I am in! I know in my heart of hearts that what I am going through is an "aggravation," not a real "problem." I know that there are people out there who have real problems.

Try to think of the "wounded warriors," the men and women who have missing limbs, brain damage and paralysis because of war injuries. I suspect that most of them are "sick and tired" of their situations to a degree that I can't begin to imagine. God bless them.

Try to think of the many senior citizens, especially those who are alone and poor, living like prisoners in unsafe neighborhoods, without anyone to visit them and without basic health care. I suspect most of them are "sick and tired" of their situations to a degree that I can't imagine. God bless them.

Try to think of the many trapped victims of spouse and child abuse who have nowhere to run and who are forced to live, day in and day out, in fear of their lives.! I suspect most of them are "sick and tired" of their situations to a degree that I can't imagine. God bless them.

Try to think of the many children who are bullied every day of their lives, crying themselves to sleep with worry about how to navigate their next day! I think of the shame, fear and powerlessness they feel, often in silence. I suspect most of them are "sick and tired" of their situations to a degree that I can't imagine. God bless them.

Try to think of those who are seriously addicted to drugs or alcohol and feel they have to sell their dignity in a host of ways just to keep going. The shame, pain and fear that most of them are drowning in is something they feel they can't shake. I suspect most of them are "sick and tired" of their situations to a degree that I can't imagine. God bless them.

Try to think of those unemployed families who live from hand to mouth every day, worrying where their next meal will come from, what they will do if one of the children gets sick or where they will live if they are evicted. I suspect most of them are "sick and tired" of their situations to a degree that I can't imagine. God bless them.

Try to think of those battling health conditions like cancer, Parkinson and Alzheimer disease. Many of them are terrified when they think of what's coming next for them. I suspect most of them are "sick and tired" of their situations to a degree that I can't imagine. God bless them.

I try to think of my many friends and acquaintances down in the Caribbean missions who struggle with employment, food, education, travel and health issues. I suspect most of them are "sick and tired" of those situations to a degree that I can't imagine. God bless them.

When all is said and done, I really have nothing to complain about.

I am still "simply amazed - forever grateful!"

Getting Tired of Extremism

> "Extremism is so easy. You've got your position, and that's it. It doesn't take much thought. And when you go far enough to the right you meet the same idiots coming around from the left."
> – Clint Eastwood, Interview,
> Time Magazine, February 20, 2005

I have always heard that we cry out in pain at both ends of life - when we come in and when we go out, when we are born and when we die.

I am one to believe that all the "crying out in pain" that keeps getting louder and louder each day is both the birth of something new and the death of something old. It's like the image of an egg that I have used often in my preaching. One day we woke up to find thin cracks in the church starting to manifest all over it. Each day the cracks keep becoming more numerous and more obvious. As this happens, some panic and do what they can to try to tape it all back together. They are convinced that we are falling apart. I know from raising chickens that the worst thing you can do when an egg starts to crack like that is to tape it back together. I believe that what one needs to do, in such cases, is to stand back and let it hatch. I can't join those who believe that we are falling apart. Rather, I choose to stand firmly with those who believe that we are simply giving birth once again - *ecclesia semper reformanda*, "the church is always in need of reform."

I believe something similar is happening in our culture. In a panic, we are engaging in "culture wars." Some of us believe that we are dying and others believe that we are giving birth. Those who are most fearful are desperately trying to make true what they love. Those who are most hopeful are desperately trying to love the new truth.

In times like ours, I suggest we resists embracing one extreme or the other, but try to stay in the sane center, working to save what is valuable while being open to innovation and change. The sane center need not be about watering down the truth, accepting mediocrity or compromising principles, but about embracing what is true in both extremes. As long as it is good, true, right and respectful, why not embrace it? Only the sowing of evil, hate, division and cruelty need to be rejected.

Why can't we value self-reliance and take care of the weak? Why can't we appreciate science and religion? Why can't we embrace the gifts of women and men. Why can't we blend the wisdom of the old and the creativity of the young? Why can't we be both passionate and flexible? Why can't we appreciate the faith of St. Paul and the doubts of St. Thomas, the prodigality of the younger son and the fidelity of the older son, the Jewish convert and the Gentile convert? Why can't we accept the fact that Democrats and Republicans both have something to add?

It doesn't have to be either/or. It can be both/and. We can proudly make our case without having to overstate it. We can honor the case that others proudly make without the need to silence them.

Traditionalists and progressives both need to heed the words of Thomas Merton. "Those who are not humble hate their past and push it out of sight, just as they cut down the growing and green things that spring up inexhaustibly even in the present."

Personally, I am trying to be like the "householder" in the gospel according to Matthew (13:51-53) who can "bring out of his storeroom things both new and old!" That passage refers to Matthew's attempt to wed the old Jewish traditions to the new reality of Jesus for Christian converts.

ENTROPY AND SENESCENCE
Just Two Fancy Words for Falling Apart

I remind you to fan into flame the gift of God that you have. For God did not give us a spirit of cowardice, but rather of power and love and self-control.
II Timothy 1:6-7

Here is a handy word you need to remember - entropy! Entropy is that natural, spontaneous and unremitting process of decline, decay and disorder unless there is an opposing force working against it.

Anyone who owns a home knows that it will fall into ruin pretty quickly without regular maintenance and constant upkeep. One of the hardest points to get across in marriage preparation programs is the point that just because you are "in love" today and promise to "be true to you in good times and bad," does not mean your marriage will survive without constant care and maintenance. Most marriages that fall apart, fall apart because of neglect. America has a major problem with obesity, but many have not figured out yet that weight cannot be managed in our culture without constant attention to diet and exercise. Many people just "let themselves go" until there is a health crisis or it's too late. Gardens need weeding. Friendships needs cultivating. Professionals need continuing education. Even our faith, unattended, is subject to withering on the vine. Entropy is that natural, spontaneous and unremitting process of decline, decay and disorder unless there is an opposing force working against it.

"Senescence" is the process of becoming old or the state of being old. As we age, we "senesce." We can't stop it, but we can challenge it. We can do a few things to slow it down. Here I am reminded of the famous poem, *Do Not Go Gentle into That Good Night*, by Dylan Thomas.

> Do not go gentle into that good night,
> Old age should burn and rave at close of day;
> Rage, rage against the dying of the light.
>
> Though wise men at their end know dark is right,
> Because their words had forked no lightning they
> Do not go gentle into that good night.
>
> Good men, the last wave by, crying how bright
> Their frail deeds might have danced in a green bay,
> Rage, rage against the dying of the light.
>
> Wild men who caught and sang the sun in flight,
> And learn, too late, they grieved it on its way,
> Do not go gentle into that good night.
>
> Grave men, near death, who see with blinding sight
> Blind eyes could blaze like meteors and be gay,
> Rage, rage against the dying of the light.

And you, my father, there on the sad height,
Curse, bless, me now with your fierce tears, I pray.
Do not go gentle into that good night.
Rage, rage against the dying of the light.

No known substance can extend life, but here are some useful tips for improving the chances of living a long time and staying healthy:

- Eat a balanced diet including five helpings of fruits and vegetables a day.

- Exercise regularly (check with a doctor before starting an exercise program).

- Get regular health check-ups.

- Don't smoke (it's never too late to quit).

- Practice safety habits at home to prevent falls and fractures.

- Always wear your seatbelt in a car.

- Stay in contact with family and friends.

- Stay active through work, play, and community.

- Avoid overexposure to the sun and the cold

- If you drink, moderation is the key.

- When you drink, let someone else drive.

- Keep personal and financial records in order to simplify budgeting and investing.

- Plan long-term housing and money needs.

- Keep a positive attitude toward life.

- Do things that make you happy.

The word "senescence" derives from the Latin "senex," meaning "old." "Senile" and "senior" come from the same root, as does "senate" which dates back to ancient Rome where the "Senatus" was originally a "council of elders" composed of the heads of patrician families.

IN THE STILLNESS
Just Before the Condo Air Conditioners Start Roaring

There is a whole lot about this pandemic that really gets on my nerves - things like having to think about going out in public places and being in crowds of people, not to mention a de facto ban on travel. On the other hand, I find myself finding new and interesting ways to enjoy being at home by myself.

One of my very favorite new things to do is to set the alarm to get up early, just before the sun starts to come up, and go out on my deck with a cup of coffee.

I like to start by just sitting there listening, first to the absence of loud sounds, then to the birds as they wake up and start their chirping. I never thought about birds waking up, but they do. At first there is one or two, then little by little there are more and finally their chirps grow louder and louder into a chorus. You wouldn't notice unless you were listening intently. It's the same with the traffic. At first the street is almost empty, then there is a car or two, then several and then a whole line of them at the traffic light.

I like it better when it is the quietest, but as the silence fades into the noise of a morning in full bloom, I like to open my i-phone app and read Morning Prayer and the Mass readings of the day. For this, I sometimes have a second cup of coffee. By this time, the silence has been drowned out by the noise of a busy morning.

Recently, enjoying this new ritual, I got up at 4:30. A gentle rain was falling on the pond below my deck. The quiet was even quieter. The temperature was "heavenly" as I sat there, with coffee in hand, soaking it up. I was suddenly reminded of an old song from years ago sung by Peter, Paul and Mary - *In the Early Morning Rain*.

When I begin this newly discovered early morning ritual, I often think about how right the Trappist monks down in Gethsemani have been all those years. Even at 6:00 in the morning when I step out on the deck, they have already been up for three hours, singing and praying and reflecting in silence.

As they know, and I have rediscovered during this pandemic, the very early morning hours have a magic about them. You hear things you never hear during the day. You see things you never notice during the day.

I am reminded of an old song I used to use to open my weekly radio program in Monticello, Kentucky, back around 1975. It is a Christian hymn written by Eleanor Farjeon in 1931, but made popular by Cat Stevens in 1971.

> Morning has broken like the first morning
> Blackbird has spoken like the first bird
> Praise for the singing. Praise for the morning
> Praise for them springing fresh from the Word.

Sweet the rain's new fall, sunlit from heaven
Like the first dew fall on the first grass
Praise for the sweetness of the wet garden
Sprung in completeness where His feet pass.

Mine is the sunlight
Mine is the morning
Born of the One Light Eden saw play
Praise with elation, praise every morning,
God's recreation of the new day.

When It's Time to Let It Go

God, I believe, is responsible for calling me to one of the "helping professions." After fifty years into it, I have learned one very important lesson - one I tend to forget every once in a while and have to be slapped awake again. *Wanting* to help people is one thing. People *wanting to be helped* is another.

Just recently, I was sitting on my deck with a friend, sharing my frustrations of trying to help people down in the islands. At the end of my litany of woes, he looked me in the eye and said, "You can't change those people!" While I am not ready to give up, it was another one of those reality slaps across my consciousness. I have never set out to change the whole country, but if I can change one life it will have been worth it! I'm still processing his words. I need to admit that I was causing my own problem by maybe wanting to fix too much too fast. Obviously, I will need more patience.

What made it so jolting was the fact that I had just come from a funeral of an old friend whose wife had reached the end of her rope trying to reach out to his children from a previous marriage. No matter what she did, it was not working. Every outreach had been rejected, but she was still trying. I spent quite a bit of time trying to get her to let go and take "no" for an answer. She was causing her own problem by wanting too much to be accepted by them. I am confident that, in time, she will learn to accept their "no," let them go and move on with her life.

Years ago, when I was a young priest, I was assigned to work with a religious Sister. No matter what I did to try to work amicably with her, it was rejected. I assumed that I had just not come up with the right approach so I tried and tried again. I took my situation to a group counseling session. After presenting the stalemate to the group, I kept saying to them, "Maybe if I tried this? Maybe if I tried that?" The more I talked, the more they laughed. Finally, one of them shouted forcefully, "When are you going to take "no" for an answer? She doesn't want to work with you!" I had to realize that I was causing my own problem by wanting her to work with me too much! I had to accept "no" for an answer, let her go her own way and move on with my life.

Most of my life, I wanted a problematic acquaintance to be different from the way he was! It wasn't till I was thirty-seven years old that I finally accepted the fact that he was not going to change and that I was going to have to live without the change I wanted! I was stuck in one of those situations where I believed that if I did not like something long enough, it would go away. I had to realize that I was causing my own problem. I had to finally accept "no," "let it go" and move on with my life.

Behind each one of those predicaments is a situation that the one who wants to help did not cause and cannot fix from the outside. The door knob of change is on the other side of the door and no matter how much one begs them to open the door, if they don't want to open the door or see a need to open the door, they won't! That leaves one with two options. You can wait till they are ready or you can just move on and let them be! Either way, you need to quite knocking on the door demanding they open it for you.

People Watching

If your right eye causes you to sin, tear it out and throw it away. It is better for you to lose one of your members than to have your whole body thrown into Gehenna.
                    Matthew 5:29

We all do it. We are constantly watching other people in the privacy of our own minds, but have you ever watched how you watch? Have you ever thought about what you are thinking about the people you are looking at?

Have you ever noticed yourself judging, evaluating, measuring or even lusting after them in your heart? "She's way too fat. She must eat everything in sight." "That is the ugliest tattoo I have ever seen! It must be homemade." "Why in the world would anyone that old be dressing like that?" "She really is beautiful, but she has a nasty disposition." "He must work out everyday to have a body like that. Too bad his teeth are crooked and rotten." "My God! Where did she get that outfit? Walmart?" "Wow! If I were going bald, I don't think I would wear a hairpiece if I couldn't afford a better one than that. It looks like a dead cat sitting on his head!" "I think if I were that fat, I would not wear such tight clothes." "I wonder where they got the money to buy a car like that? Probably from selling drugs or borrowing the money on extended credit."

To be honest, I have to admit that I have caught myself engaged in judging, evaluating and measuring people! Doing those things is a bad habit that I am intentionally trying to correct. I am still "people watching," but I am trying to do it with a different outlook. I bless them! I try to think of all they are probably dealing with and I wish them well and pray that they will thrive and flourish in life.

The other evening, I watched the sidewalk along Eastern Parkway in front of my condo. There was a woman walking up the hill to the bus stop. I imagined she was a worker at the nursing home down the street on her way home. I imagined her being exhausted from a bus ride that morning and a long day of changing adult diapers at the nursing home. I imagined her having another long bus ride home, cooking supper for her family, doing laundry and maybe even having to face an abusive husband and the care of several dependent children. I wished her well! I sent all the positive energy I could muster. I prayed that God would take care of her, that she had friends who could encourage her and that she would have health good enough to sustain her.

One afternoon last week, I looked out at the sidewalk. I saw a couple of teenagers walking, talking and laughing with each other. They were quite loud about it. Instead of being irritated at their noise, I wished them all the happiness they could handle. I prayed they would be successful in life, protected from drug abuse, poverty and disease. I hoped they would live a long life and grow up to be excellent parents and contributing citizens.

Another day, I saw a young girl, over-weight, tattooed, nose pierced and green-dyed hair. She had squeezed into some skin-tight pants - or at least she tried to! At first, I thought to myself, "how pathetic!" Then I realized that she was probably a very lonely soul, desperately wanting to fit in and wanting to be trendy like "other girls." I imagined her being teased, laughed at and verbally abused by cruel peers. I sent her a spiritual hug and asked God to protect her, help her find peace of mind and let her know that she was valuable in his eyes...and hopefully in the eyes of some significant others.

Last week, I became outraged at the people who were gathering in large close groups, without masks, and risking not only their health, but the health of those they would come in contact with later on! At first, I was becoming angrier and angrier by the moment. I think I even called them "selfish dumb-asses" under my breath. Then I stopped and tried to think of them as simply "ignorant" and "not knowing any better!" I prayed they would be protected and I prayed that those they would come into contact with would be protected as well! I prayed that God would help them "wake up" and realize how much pain they could bring to themselves and those they love - maybe even to their parents and grandparents.

In a world where selfish, rude, crude and crass behavior is becoming a norm, the practice of "blessing people" is becoming harder and harder to do. We may not be able to change other people's public behavior, but we can try to change ours - choosing not to become mean and nasty in our responses. If we can't change them, at least we don't have to join them.

Do I Hear a Ringing in My Ears?

Jesus got into a boat and his disciples followed him. Suddenly a violent storm came up on the sea, so that the boat was being swamped by waves; but he was asleep. They came and woke him, saying, "Lord, save us! We are perishing!" He said to them, "Why are you terrified, O you of little faith?" Then he got up, rebuked the winds and the sea, and there was great calm. The men were amazed and said, "What sort of man is this, whom even the winds and the sea obey?"
                                Matthew 8

> *For Whom the Bell Tolls*
> John Donne

> No man is an island,
> Entire of itself.
> Each is a piece of the continent,
> A part of the main.
> If a clod be washed away by the sea,
> Europe is the less.
> As well as if a promontory were.
> As well as if a manor of thine own
> Or of thine friend's were.

> Each man's death diminishes me,
> For I am involved in mankind.
> Therefore, send not to know
> For whom the bell tolls,
> It tolls for thee.

I have got to start restricting myself to the amount of TV news I watch! All day, every day, it's one "breaking news" story after the next, giving us the number of "new COVID cases," the latest "number of deaths" and how many "overflow morgues" have been set up.

I am not one to panic, normally, but with that kind of information coming into my psyche every day, I am beginning to "lose it." I use to imagine that I would die in my own bed, on clean sheets, propped up on pillows, with adoring relatives and friends listening to my farewell speech while writing it all down for posterity. When I let my mind run wild, I have begun to imagine that I could be one of those patients, with tubes down my throat, parked in a crowed hospital hallway, with doctors and nurses too busy to even notice. As a result, I have my "end of life" papers laying out for easy access in an emergency.

I am still hoping that I can escape this COVID-19 virus, but if I can't I can only hope I don't end up in one of those busy hospital hallways, hooked to tubes, with no one with time enough to help me. Of course, I have always hoped I'd win the lottery, but that hasn't happened! On the other hand, I guess, since I have not been infected yet, I have already won the lottery for that matter! If I do end up like that, I am beginning to think I may ask them to give me some good drugs and send me home to die in peace.

Jesus was right, "fear is useless, what is needed is trust." I need to quit watching so much "breaking news" and put my focus on other people - especially the ones who are actually suffering in this pandemic, not just those of us who are afraid of suffering.

The Peace of Wild Things
Wendell Berry

When despair for the world grows in me
and I wake in the night at the least sound
in fear of what my life and my children's lives
    may be,
I go and lie down where the wood drake
rests in his beauty on the water, and the great
    heron feeds.
I come into the peace of wild things
who do not tax their lives with forethought
of grief. I come into the presence of still water.
And I feel above me the day-blind stars
waiting with their light. For a time
I rest in the grace of the world, and am free.

Home Alone

Eleanor Rigby

Ah, look at all the lonely people
Ah, look at all the lonely people

Eleanor Rigby
Picks up the rice in the church where a wedding
    has been
Lives in a dream
Waits at the window
Wearing the face that she keeps in a jar by the door
Who is it for?

All the lonely people
Where do they all come from?
All the lonely people
Where do they all belong?

Father McKenzie
Writing the words of a sermon that no one
    will hear
No one comes near
Look at him working
Darning his socks in the night when there's
    nobody there
What does he care?

All the lonely people
Where do they all come from?

All the lonely people
Where do they all belong?

Ah, look at all the lonely people
Ah, look at all the lonely people

Eleanor Rigby
Died in the church and was buried along with
   her name
Nobody came
Father McKenzie
Wiping the dirt from his hands as he walks
   from the grave
No one was saved

All the lonely people (ah, look at all the
   lonely people)
Where do they all come from?
All the lonely people (ah, look at all the
   lonely people)
Where do they all belong?

                SONG WRITERS: John Lennon/PaulMcCartney

    The day I drafted this blog post, I had not been out of the house all day - for several days in fact - but I never felt lonely. It was because nine people called or wrote to me just that day. In a typical day, I may be here alone, but I am certainly not without human contact. Their calls, cards, texts and lunch invitations validate the words, "The worst feeling isn't being lonely... it's being forgotten." It was comforting to know that I may be out of people's sight, but I am not out of people's hearts and minds! For that, I am "simply amazed and forever grateful!"

Having a Safe Place to Live

My refuge and fortress, my God in whom I trust.

God's faithfulness is a protecting shield.
Psalm 91:2,4

During this pandemic, it is very easy to focus on all the bad things that are happening - sickness, unemployment, racial unrest, nasty personal behaviors of all kinds and even death.

As an alternative to being overly focused on all that, I am making a deliberate effort to do two things - focus on the needs of others and focus on the things for which I need to be grateful.

The other day, I heard there was a tropical storm heading right for Saint Vincent and the Grenadines where I have been volunteering for the last five years. I thought of the mudslides that I have seen covering the roads after lots of rain. I thought about all those mountainside shacks that I have passed many times when I have been down there. I thought of the poor families living in them during a tropical storm, scared that a mudslide might engulf them or scared that their home could collapse around them any minute and everything they own could be swept away, leaving them dead in some ravine never to be seen again. I keep asking myself, "what is it like not having a safe place to live?"

I thought about all those people, one pay check away from eviction, wondering what in the world their families would do if they were asked to leave their rented homes. I have never had to think about being kicked out of the home I lived in because it belonged to someone else and I could not afford to pay them for the right to live there! Some of them have been going through that anxiety every month for years. Some of them have had to move more times than they can probably remember. I keep asking myself, "what is it like not having a safe place to live?"

It crossed my mind at some point that some people are forced to live in terror of physical, verbal, psychological and sexual abuse. For them, their house is not a "home," but a prison, a psych ward and a torture chamber with no escape route. I keep asking myself, "what is it like not having a safe place to live?"

I try to imagine what it would be like to live in a dangerous, high-crime area, where people have to sleep with one eye open and a gun or knife under their pillow in case of a home invasion, where people have to listen to shouting and cursing most of the night, where people are afraid to go outside even during the day or open their door to anyone who knocks? I keep asking myself, "what is it like not having a safe place to live?"

Then I look around my roomy, Germantown, paid-for, air-conditioned, secure condo and I realize how blessed I am! When I go to bed an night, I know that I will sleep peacefully and secure and with nothing really to worry about! When I really take the time to think of others, I am filled with a sense of gratitude. I realize again that my little "aggravations" are not really "problems" so surely I can at least give up complaining. When I go to bed at night, expecting a peaceful restful sleep, I pray for those who do not have that luxury in their lives. I ask God to protect them from harm. I ask God to help me break the habit of "making mountains out of molehills" because I know what it is like to have a safe place to live.

Leaving a Legacy

I will prove myself worthy of my old age, and I will leave to the young an example of how to die willingly and generously for the revered and holy law.
                                II Maccabees 6:28

I don't think I obsess about it, but it occurred to me the other day that during this pandemic I have thought about, and wrote about, death quite often! Much of it has to do with the fact that death is in the headline news everyday. Along with that, in the last month or two, I have been called on to do four grave-side services which has contributed to my thinking about death as well. All this, along with reaching the age of seventy-six, has led me to realize that death has become a point of reflection that I need to embrace on a personal level. If all that is not enough, the other day I got some help from the Chancery Office. They sent me papers to fill out, telling me that it was time for me to update my funeral and end-of-life plans!

In my reflections, I have thought often of old Eleazar in the Old Testament. Eleazar was a very old Jewish man who was given the choice of eating pork against the teachings of his sacred faith or be killed. He could have saved his life by "going along." His friends even tried to help him devise a scheme where he merely "appeared" to eat pork. He made up his mind to remain loyal to the holy laws of God and reject any efforts to "fake it."

His reasons are worth quoting directly. "At our age it would be unbecoming to make such a pretense; many young men would think the ninety-year old Eleazar had gone over to an alien religion. Should I thus dissimulate for the sake of a brief moment of life, they would be led astray by me, while I bring shame and dishonor on my old age."

"Even if for the time being, I avoid the punishment of men, I shall never, whether alive or dead, escape the hands of the Almighty. Therefore, by manfully giving up my life now, I will prove myself worthy of my old age, and I will leave to the young a noble example of how to die willingly and generously for the revered and holy laws." (II Maccabees 6:24-28)

In my reflections, the word "legacy" came to mind. A legacy is something that a person leaves behind by which they can be remembered. When you don't have children, an established charitable foundation or a public monument dedicated in your honor, what can your legacy be?

As for my own legacy, the words of Shannon Alder might be a good place to start. "Carve your name on hearts, not tombstones. A legacy is etched into the minds of others and the stories they share about you." The only part of that sentiment that really scares me to death is the part "the stories they share about you!" However, Oscar Wilde may have been right when he said, "There is only one thing in the world worse than being talked about, and that is not being talked about."

The legacy I wish to leave behind may be outlined in one line of an old prayer that I said almost every week when I visited the nursing home. It is called "Learning Christ." It is a prayer that a dear friend, Marea Gardner, introduced me to in her final days. This one line always stood out for me. "May no one be less good for having come within my influence." Yes, that's it! I want my legacy to be the fact that the people who crossed my path left better off.

My prayer, then, going forward can be summed up in the words of that prominent Quaker missionary from the early 1800s, Stephen Grellet. "I shall pass through this world but once. Any good therefore that I can do or any kindness that I can show to any human being, let me do it now. Let me not defer or neglect it, for I shall not pass this way again."

"What will you leave behind?" Since I don't have children, I probably will not leave much! However, I do like to think that some of my "encouraging words" might continue to live on for a while after I am gone because I took the time to publish them in little spiritual reading books. In my home, I have a wall of framed book covers that I have been calling my "baby pictures."

It's not the number of books that count, however, it is the "encouraging words" in them that really count! The words of Maya Angelou come to mind. "I've learned that people will forget what you said, people will forget what you did, but people will never forget how you made them feel." This is the legacy I want. "He made me feel good about myself." "He always offered me an "encouraging word." "I was better off from knowing him."

Today I want to offer an encouraging word to all men and women, my age and older, as regards our "legacies" - the examples we set and leave behind for the young. For many of you, it is for your children and grandchildren. For me, it is my twenty nieces and nephews, as well as the parishioners, seminarians, friends and college students with whom I have done my ministry.

I often ask myself these days, "What will my many parishioners, nieces, nephews, seminarians, college students and friends remember about me? Have I been kind, encouraging, generous, magnanimous and affirming toward them? Will they remember me as a credible example of fidelity and practicing what I have preached?" I truly hope so because I have certainly tried.

What will your "legacy" be? What do you want it to be? You may still have time to build it up - or even repair it if necessary.

> *Whatever you can do, or dream you can, begin it. Boldness has genius, power and magic in it.*
> Wolfgang von Johann Goethe

Safety Fatigue

Let us not grow tired of doing good,
for in due time we shall reap our harvest,
if we do not give up.
Galatians 6:9

Like many other people these days, I am tired of this pandemic. It is exhausting, mentally and physically. I am tired of the anxiety, the fear of getting infected, the economic-related stress, the difficulty of handling social distancing restrictions and changes in daily life. I am tired of being cooped up, tired of being careful and tired of being scared. Sometimes I feel like just saying "to hell with this" and ignoring all the warnings. Of course, this is the very reason COVID-19 is rising sharply again in some places in the U.S - some people have grown careless about wearing masks and social distancing. For some their's is simply angry resistance.

There is research that defines the stages of stress on communities from disasters. From what I read, people like me are right on target.

Early during a disaster, communities tend to pull together, support each other and bond together. Remember the first weeks of the stay-at-home orders when everyone in the neighborhood waved at everyone else?

Eventually, that heroic spirit wears thin, stress begins to build and we hit a period of disillusionment when we lose our optimism and start having negative, angry reactions.

This seems to be where we are right now as a country. Many are exhausted by it all and have started saying to themselves, "I don't care if I get COVID-19. I would rather get sick than stay home and be careful. Because it appears that this pandemic could last a while, I am tempted, but so far I haven't given into these feelings.

There are things we can do and I have been doing some of them. First, I have been on the treadmill almost every day and I have taken walks in the cemetery near my house with a few friends. They say exercise releases endorphins and gets some of the adrenaline out when frustration builds. Second, I write and I talk to people on the phone, skype and what's app because saying it out loud helps release some of the stress. Third, what hurts more than the situation itself is how we think about the situation. I am trying to think positively by encouraging myself to "hang in there." Limiting the amount of news I watch each day helps me from drowning in the negativity and staying afloat. I need to hear the facts, but I don't need to overdose on them. I try to remind myself to take it one day at a time, to stay in the present rather than letting my mind race off into some misery-ridden future and some unretrievable past.

We don't have to seal ourselves in a bubble, but we do have to act sensibly, follow the CDC guidelines and encourage one another to "keep on keepin' on!" Most of all, realizing that we were probably moving too fast in the past, we need to learn to chill, to take it easy and to go with the flow!" I know from the experience of watching a good friend drown right in front of me that the worst thing one can do in a situation like that is to panic. The secret to surviving is learning to relax so that you can float to safety.

Trying to Keep No Enemies

Wrath and anger are hateful things, yet the sinner hugs them tight. The vengeful will suffer the Lord's vengeance, for he remembers their sins in detail. Forgive your neighbor's injustice; then when you pray, your own sins will be forgiven.
Sirach 27:30-28:2

One of the things I like to regularly is to do a quick "life review" to see if I have any enemies. During this pandemic, with a lot more time on my hands, I have had more time to think about it.

I realized years ago that having an enemy is a heavy bag of stinking garbage to carry around. Mark Twain nailed it when he said, "Anger is an acid that can do more harm to the vessel in which it is stored than to anything on which it is poured." I agree with him so much that I regularly "take stock" of whether I have any enemies and try to "love" them anyway.

I do not think I have any real "enemies" at this time, but it seems that there is always one or two people who let me know they dislike me for one reason or another.

At this time, I can only think of four people whom I would categorize as "problematic" as far as my relationship with them. Since I know hundreds and hundreds of people, I guess that's not too bad! The interesting thing about it is the fact that all four of them are priests! None of them have confronted me openly with insults or name-calling. They "punish" me with the "silent treatment." They simply do not speak to me, give me the time of day or acknowledge my existence. In trying to find out the cause of this punishing silence, I have been told that they consider me "too liberal" or they were "jealous of my visibility."

In reading about it, I found out that it is a form of abuse that is often used by narcissists, consciously or unconsciously, to make their victims feel unworthy, to deny them emotional care, to deny them praise, to starve them of love, affection, compliments and positive feedback, to regularly reject, degrade and deny them emotional responsiveness. It is a form of repetitive abuse that is aimed at controlling, diminishing another person's well-being in order to hurt, punish, harm or control them. Best of all, it can be used to control their victims by keeping them guessing! It makes sense that punishing silence is a favorite technique of narcissists. Narcissists cannot tolerate the fact that someone else might shine as bright or brighter than them! Starving their competition out makes more sense to them than sharing the limelight or attacking outright.

The person on the receiving end can end up resigned to feeling isolated, intimidated, insignificant, despondent, angry, resentful and even revengeful. Emotional stress brought about by persistent silent treatment can actually affect physical health. Some victims have noted that their abuser becomes notably happier the more worn down and miserable their victims become. In order to cope, the victim must appreciate that an abuser thrives on observing the negative effect they have on their target. Therefore it is necessary to stop "feeding' their desire for control and power. This means not giving them the satisfaction of seeing the negative emotional effects of their immature behavior. They can derive a great sense of self importance and triumph if you get irate, annoyed, upset, capitulate, apologize, weep or plead with them to talk to you. The best thing to do is to starve them of these rewards! Meanwhile, they can always tell themselves they did nothing, said nothing and therefore are free of any blame.

In my reflection, I have come to admit that, in these cases, I am part of the problem! I let these people "get to me" because I hold a few of Albert's Ellis's "Irrational and Dysfunctional Beliefs." Here are two of those irrational beliefs that regularly cause me pain. BELIEF #1. "It is a dire necessity for adult humans to be loved or approved of by virtually every significant other person in their community." BELIEF #2. "People absolutely must act considerately and fairly and they are damnable villains if they do not. He called it "awfulizing" as in "ain't it awful."

When you hold those irrational beliefs, you are bound to be "let down" over and over again! The secret is not giving their negativity attention. You just have to "let them go" and let them "feel whatever they feel." Most of all, do not allow yourself to turn them into an "enemy." That would give them even more power over you.

Standing on Holy Ground

Since we are surrounded by so great a cloud of witnesses, let us persevere in running the race that lies before us while keeping our eyes fixed on Jesus.
Hebrews 12:1-4

During this pandemic, I have had at least four graveside funeral services, rather than traditional funeral Masses inside a church. As I prepared a homily for my first cousin who was buried in Saint Mary Magdalen Church in Payneville, Kentucky, I was struck by the fact that cemeteries are called "consecrated" ground for a reason. Here are some of the thoughts I shared with the people who attended his funeral.

My dear family and friends! We are standing on holy ground! We are surrounded by a cloud of witnesses – those who have gone before us after they have completed their time here on earth! Our parents, siblings, uncles and aunts, our neighbors, our friends and our fellow parishioners are buried here! Yes, this is holy ground! Here lie the relics of some powerful saints with whom we share DNA and endless memories.

Yes, make no mistake about it! This is holy ground and we are surrounded by a cloud of witness who have faithfully lived the Christian faith in this community. They were good, good, good people! If most of them are not saints by now, then I don't have much of a chance! Let's be clear about one thing! We are burying another family member in holy ground.

As I was preparing this homily, I thought of a reliquary that someone gave me a few years ago. It is a large, gold locket with a small door containing a tiny bone fragment of Saint Pius X. A "reliquary" then is something that holds the bones of a saint. This cemetery, this holy ground that we stand on today, is really one big "reliquary." It holds the bones of this community's saints – the bones of our saints.

Many of you might remember the thriller film, *The Sixth Sense*, which tells the story of Cole Sear, a troubled, isolated boy, who is able to see and talk to the dead, and an equally troubled child psychologist (played by Bruce Willis), who tries to help him. The most famous line from the film belong to the young boy. "I see dead people."

In a way, that is exactly what the writer of the Letter to the Hebrews, that I read from today, is telling us when he says, "we are surrounded by a "cloud of witnesses." In fact, he is saying four things.

First, he is telling us that living the Christian life is like running a race. It is not a stroll for the lazy and indifferent. It takes the serious discipline of an athlete. We have to train every day of our lives. We have to know where we are going, remain focused, and keep our eyes on the finish line.

Second, he is telling us that there are people "in the stands," people who have run the race before us and who have already crossed the finish line, who are cheering us on! Can't you feel their presence right now! This fact challenges us to remember that we are surrounded by a large group of supportive onlookers as we live out our lives as Christians. This is precisely what we mean when we say in our Creed that we believe in the "communion of the saints." That is so damned easy to say, but today, standing here, I feel it! I, for one, do not actually see dead people, but I do feel their presence, helping me along the way. I believe that I am not alone on my journey of faith, but I am part of a larger story, a great procession of people marching through history.

Third, he is telling us to "persevere in running the race that lies before us." Dropping out of the race is always an option, especially for the college students I used to work with when I was chaplain at Bellarmine University. . One of the big questions before the college students I worked with is this one. "Will you abandon the religious upbringing of your childhood or will you choose it for myself of your own free will? Will you persevere in living your Catholic Christian faith or will you simply drop out of the race because it is too hard, because it is too much trouble, because it demands too much, because it is too inconvenient or because others around you are dropping out as well?

Fourth, he is telling us to "keep our eyes fixed on Jesus." Distractions are a problem for all of us, no matter how many laps of the race we have completed. There are those who seek to draw our attention away from the race we are running. "Look here! Look over there! Look at me! Look at this! Pay attention to this! Pay attention to that! See this! See that!" If we are to persevere in running this race, we must keep our eyes fixed on the finish line, we must "keep our eyes fixed on Jesus." As we stand here among our family saints, let us be reminded, in the starkest way possible, that we too will be lying with them someday! We will then be part of this "cloud of witnesses." We must remain focused on what we are doing and why we are doing, until we hear Jesus say to us at the finish line, "Well done, good and faithful servant, enter into the joy of your master!"

I hope that you have had the time to share your favorite stories about our dear cousin. In your own way, you have shared short "eulogies" about him with each other. "Eulogies" are stories about what the deceased did for God – his professional accomplishments, his educational achievements, his services to the community and his dedication to his family.

"Eulogies" are popular these days at funerals, but when we list all that the deceased did, we have to be careful. We cannot list them and then conclude that the deceased "earned his way to heaven" by doing all those good deeds. No, they must be seen as a grateful response to God's free gift of salvation! Nobody can earn salvation! It's free for the taking! We can't earn it and we don't deserve it, but God gives it to us free of charge.

Priests and deacons, when they speak at funerals, are instructed not to give "eulogies" for that reason. It could give a wrong impression that salvation can be earned by good deeds! They are instructed to give a "homily." What's the difference? A "eulogy" is all about what the deceased did for God! A "eulogy" is all about what God did for the deceased.

I had the honor of hearing my cousin's confession, anointing him and giving him "communion" - "viaticum." "Viaticum" is communion for those who are dying. It means "something you take with you on the way - a packed lunch, if you will!" It is bread for his journey through death to new life - the very Body of Christ himself. Our cousin may not have been a "living saint" while he was here on earth, none of us are, but I believe he is now a "living saint" in heaven, not because of his goodness, but because of God's goodness.

When this pandemic gets you down, take a walk through a cemetery. Let that "holy ground" remind you of where you came from, where you are now and where you are headed! Let it remind you that you are not walking alone, but that you are surrounded by a great cloud of witnesses cheering you on toward the finish line.

Dragging On

Anxiety in one's heart weighs a person down.
Proverbs 12:25

This pandemic is dragging on and on with no end in sight! I suppose this is what Father Joe White, Rector of Saint Thomas Seminary, was feeling about me in 1964 when he yelled out in front of my whole class "Knott! You have been a ball and chain around my leg for six years!" He might have just said, "When will you get the hell out of here?" I couldn't say anything back in those days, but the feelings were mutual! He was more of a ball and chain around my entire psyche! Both of us longed for the day to say "good riddance" to each other as the years dragged on and on.

You say an event or process "drags on" when you disapprove of the fact that it lasts far longer than necessary. I say I am sick of dealing with this pandemic but my disapproval is having little effect on it so I guess I am going to have to find a way to live around it, if not with it! It is what it is, whether I like it or not, so the only question left is, "What am I going to do now?"

The first thing, of course, is to face facts. Stuff happens, and often difficult stuff happens that we not only didn't see coming, didn't do anything to deserve, and have no control over much less be able to stop. When we refuse to accept what is happening, we produce more anxiety and stress. Then, not only do we have a bad situation on our hands, but we end up making things worse by creating sleeplessness, muscle tension and mood swings.

Part of facing facts, is to realize that although we can't change what is happening, we are not completely powerless. We can choose how we want to react to what we can't control. We can do that by talking things over with our friends, family members or even a therapist. Just "talking it out" helps a lot of people. I choose to do that sometimes, but more often than not, I do what I am doing right - I write! I write about my feelings! Seeing them expressed on paper and reading over them helps me process those feelings. Sometimes, they even help others process their feelings when I am able to share what I write. Journaling has been helpful to many, many people working through their unpleasant feelings.

If you catch yourself sounding like a "victim," or others start pointing out that you are sounding too much like a victim, you can choose to change courses and choose operating out of your power. Instead of being overly focused on all the things you can't do, you can start focusing on all the things that you can do.

Here, never underestimate the benefits of a good disaster! You will be shocked by how many benefits this pandemic has offered you if you change your perspective. For example, your staying home more gives you the opportunity to create a cleaner house! Your not eating out and shopping so much can save you a whole lot of money! Your lack of a social life has given you more opportunities to connect with neglected family members and old friends by phone, face-time, e-mail, texting or whats app. You may have been eating too much fast food. This time has given you the opportunity to cook again, try new recipes and create family meals together. You may not have felt the need, or had the time to pray, before now. You may now feel the need and have time to do something about it! This slower pace has given you time to take more walks, get out that old bicycle, turn on that old treadmill or hike in the woods. Any of that is better than feeling sorry for yourself amidst the reality of this damnable pandemic.

The list goes on and on, if you change your focus and become more imaginative! Good things can happen even in the midst of bad things.

From Excluded to Included

Go therefore to the crossroads and invite to the banquet as many as you can find. So the servants went out into the streets and gathered everyone they could find, both good and bad alike, and the wedding hall was filled with guests.
Matthew 22:10

There is such a thing as a problem within a problem. The pandemic is wearing on me, but behind it is something that is wearing on me even more! The "other something" is that constant drumbeat of some people looking for opportunities to exclude others instead of looking for ways to include them.

The news is full of stories about racial injustice, anti-dreamer legislation, the political demonization of other points of view, ageism, sexism, anti-sexual orientation rhetoric, anti-science movements, climate denial, voter suppression, economic greed and ignored corruption. I believe it all comes from the fear of shortages and simple ignorance. The fear of shortages is basically a fear that there will not be enough for all of us, so I've got to protect what's coming to me. The "ignorance response" is basically a fear of having to revise one's map of reality to include new realities - if I don't know about it, it can't affect me.

What makes me so sensitive to those "who's in/who's out" walls that some people always seem to be wanting to erect is that growing up I was on the outside most of the time looking for a way to get inside. Feeling excluded was a familiar feeling as a child, teenager and young adult.

As a child, in frustration, my father would often let us know, in no uncertain terms that we were a burden to him and that we were losers. "I'll be glad when you kids are grown and out of here!" "You'll never amount to a hill of beans!"

In grade school, I was so thin and small that I was teased about being a "runt." A "runt" was the last of the baby pigs to be born leaving it undersized and unable to fight the stronger ones for a place to nurse. "Runts" usually died.

In minor seminary, in the suburbs of Kentucky's largest city, being born and raised in the country subjected us to the ridicule of the urban-born seminarians. "You hillbillies! You hicks!"

In the early days of priesthood, I served in the home missions of our diocese where Catholics were only one-tenth of one-percent. Being Catholic was like being a leper! People avoided you, whispered about you and snubbed you on a regular basis.

I used to think all this was a curse and a burden to bear. However, what it was actually doing was preparing me for my major life's work - reaching out to and embracing the marginal of this world.

As the pastor of the Cathedral, I got the chance to revitalize the that parish by reaching out mainly to marginal Catholics: those who had fallen away from practicing their faith, divorced Catholics, gay and lesbian Catholics, the poor, immigrants and various other minorities. We grew from about 110 members to 2100 members in a 14 year period. While those who responded to our invitation, "we'll take anybody," were delighted to be included, there was a handful of mean people who wanted me to reject, condemn and shame those people lest I be known for "approving sin."

When I am "inclusive" in my words and my deeds, I believe I have been on solid ground as a Christian. Does the Book of Genesis (1:27) not say, "so God created man in His own image, in the image of God He created him, male and female he created him. Did Jesus not teach us powerfully, in his central parables, about rejoicing over the lost sheep, the lost coin and the lost son?

When I am "inclusive" in my words and in my deeds, I believe I have been on solid ground as a Catholic." Does the very word "catholic" not means "universal" and "inclusive." We are not some American church. We are a church made up of people from every race, language and way of life on this planet.

When I am "inclusive" in my words and in my deeds, I believe I have been on solid ground as an American. Does the Constitution itself not say, "We hold these truths to be self-evident, that all men are created equal, that they are endowed by their creator with certain unalienable Rights, that among these are Life, Liberty and the pursuit of Happiness?" Does the Statute of Liberty not proclaim for all the world to see, "Give me your tired, your poor, your huddled masses yearning to breathe free, the wretched refuse of your teeming shore. Send these, the homeless, tempest-tossed to me. I lift my lamp beside the golden door."

Oh God! Deliver me from the fear of shortages and new realities. Help me keep my mind, heart and arms open, even when it hurts and becomes personally inconvenient.

Walking on Thin Ice

We walk by faith, not by sight.
II Corinthians 6:7

Some of my favorite TV shows are the ones featuring people living in the backwoods of Alaska: *Life Below Zero, Mountain Men, Alaska the Last Frontier, The Last Alaskans, 100 Days Wild, Alaskan Bush People* and *Yukon Men*. One of the regular hazards, other than being attacked by bears, is falling through thin ice when trying to cross a river. Very often they refer to children, neighbors, spouses and friends who have fallen through the ice only to be swept to their deaths in a flash.

"Walking on thin ice," "treading on thin ice" or "skating on thin ice" are familiar expressions we use to refer to the various precarious situations in which we find ourselves. It occurred to me the other day how "on target" those expressions are when I think about how I feel almost every day of this pandemic - especially during quiet reflective moments. They express that tenuous feeling that many of us have about the possibility of being swept to our deaths before we know it.

"Walking on thin ice" can refer to two distinct things. It can refer to the foolhardiness of taking the risk of walking out on thin ice as a silly dare from a bunch of drunken teenagers! It can, however, refer to the courage of taking the risk of walking out on thin ice as a way to get food or medical assistance for a family close to starvation or death from a stroke.

We see both types of "walking on thin ice" being acted out during this pandemic. We see the foolhardiness of a bunch of young adults gathered, cheek to cheek, in a bar without a thought to social distancing or wearing a mask. We see the courage of health care workers courageously entering hospitals and nursing homes to care for those who have contracted the COVID-19 disease. Both are "walking on thin ice," but for two distinctly different reasons. One group is selfishly and foolishly "tempting fate" and the other group is heroically and generously "laying down their lives" in service to their fellow men and women.

Lastly, there are those of us who have a choice! We can "walk on thin ice" by being selfish and foolhardy, in a fog of denial, and put ourselves and others in jeopardy. On the other hand, we can "walk on thin ice" by embracing a less than exciting life by staying out of crowds, by wearing masks and by sanitizing our hands in an effort to slow the spread of this disease.

Golden Years Have Become Stolen Years

God will bless you, if you don't give up when your faith is being tested. He will reward you with a glorious life, just as he rewards everyone who loves him.
                                James 1:12

How many ways has this pandemic affected us as people? Let me count the ways. So far this is number twenty-nine and I am just one person.

The other day, I realized that I too am going through what Michelle Obama called a "low grade depression." Yes, that's it! I feel that behind my steely determination to "rage, rage" against this pandemic, I am always battling a little bit of depression.

I have always heard that depression is about anger that you don't know what to do with. I guess I need to admit that I am beginning to feel that this pandemic is stealing my retirement years and ruining all that I had planned to do ... and I am damn mad about it! On one level, I feel I earned it and all this seems so brutally unfair! On the other hand, I know that I am one of the lucky older ones in the great scheme of things! As a result, I am bouncing back and forth between peace and panic.

Nothing like a quick visit with someone working in a nursing home to drive my point home. The other day I was getting an update from Mother Paul at the local Little Sisters of the Poor Home for the Aged. As I was leaving, it occurred to me how "robbed" they are of even a peaceful ending to their lives! They can't even go to a nursing home and receive some basic care without it being one of the most dangerous places in the world when it comes to this pandemic.

They are robbed of the comfort of visits from their children, grandchildren and friends. The best they can get sometimes is waving to them outside of a closed window or hearing their voices over a phone. No hand holding! No hugs! No being close enough to carry on a regular conversation. Some die totally alone in the middle of the night with no one to even notice.

Even those living at home, or being cared for by their children, are robbed of simple things like a lunch out, going to church, volunteering with other seniors or shopping from their wheel chairs at the mall.

This pandemic is for me similar to a "mass mugging and robbery" of our most senior citizens. It's sad. It's unfair. It's unfortunately a reality.

Before we start feeling sorry for ourselves too much, let's put all this in perspective. Let us remember the fact that it hasn't been too many years ago that older people never got to retire or even live to a ripe old age.

CHILDHOODS ARE BEING STOLEN AS WELL

As I was finishing this blog post, it occurred to me that what I have said above could also be said of young people. Many of them are seeing their childhoods stolen by this pandemic. They have seen their classes, graduations and proms being scaled back or cancelled. Football games, spring breaks and other large gathering are becoming rarer and rarer. Many of the things that have looked forward to and dreamed about this fall are not going to happen. It's sad. It's unfair. It's unfortunately a reality for them too!

Before we start feeling sorry for ourselves too much, let's put all this in perspective. Let us remember the fact that it hasn't been too many years ago that many children never survived polio, measles, whooping cough and diphtheria to grow into healthy teenagers and young adults.

As the Days Slip Away

How long will you lie there, you lazy person?
When will you get up from sleeping?
You sleep a little; you take a nap.
You fold your hands and lie down to rest.
Proverbs 6

Have you ever been driving down the road, far from a gas station, and notice that the fuel gauge is on empty? Have you ever been traveling and notice that the battery on your cell phone is showing bars of red letting you know that it's about to go dead? Have you ever been working on your taxes as the deadline is approaching and you begin to panic as you realize that you can't get it all done? Have you ever had a ride to the airport and remember that you forgot your passport and you probably don't have time to go back and get it? Have you ever had a pile of bills in front of you and a checking account that is about to hit zero?

That's how I am beginning to feel about this pandemic. I am 76, I am retired, I have some savings tucked away, I am still in good physical condition and here I am stuck in this condo unable to travel or even leave the house without worrying about contracting a virus that could kill me! I am realizing that time is running out and there is not a damned thing I can do about it! I feel stuck. I feel powerless. I feel disappointed. I feel there could be no good ending to this situation.

I keep asking myself these questions. What would you do if you were about to run out of gas out on the road? What would you do if the battery were to go dead and you desperately needed to make a call? What would you do if the taxes were due and you didn't have time to file them? What would you do if you were on your way to the airport, with barely enough time to make it, and remembered that you forgot your passport? What would you do you with a stack of bills and no money left to pay them? What would you do if you knew that getting upset, angry and resentful wouldn't change anything? The only sensible thing to do would be to chill and let whatever is going to happen, happen. You would then try to find a way to deal with the consequences in the best way you could. In all the cases mentioned, as inconvenient as things might become, it would not be the end of the world. You would figure something out.

That is what I am trying to do during this pandemic - figure something out! Yes, I am grateful I am not sick. Yes, I am grateful I have food and housing and an adequate income. Yes, I am grateful that I have people who love me and care for me. Yes, I am grateful for so many things, but the one thing I can't seem to shake is the feeling that time is running out while I am stuck here at home, pretty much powerless to do anything about it. I used to think I had "places to go and people to see." Now I am not sure - not sure at all.

In four years, I will be eighty years old! I feel that I should be working on my "bucket list," not living like a bear in hibernation! I do pray for patience, but when my mind wraps itself around how much of the precious time I have left is being wasted waiting for this pandemic to end, I begin to really get irritated. Then I have to talk myself down from the "ledge" again - well, not a real ledge, just an emotional ledge! Thankfully, I live basement-level most of the time so I have no where to jump, but up.

In the end, all I can say is "Other people have it much worse than you, so get a grip, quit whining and deal with it, Ronald!"

IF IT AIN'T MESSY, IT AIN'T REAL

The whole congregation of the people of Israel grumbled against Moses and Aaron in the wilderness, and the people of Israel said to them, "Would that we had died by the hand of the LORD in the land of Egypt, when we sat by the meat pots and ate bread to the full, for you have brought us out into this wilderness to kill this whole assembly with hunger."
Exodus 16:1

I have never witnessed the actual birth of a child, but from every thing I have heard or seen it is a difficult and messy process. The closest thing I have come to watching the process was the birth of farm animals when I was growing up in the country. Typically, it involved a lot of pain, struggle and noise. Even the hatching of an egg was a life and death struggle for the chick. As I got older, I realized that the process of dying was similar. It often involves a lot of pain, struggle and even noise. The process of coming to life and leaving life are very similar in that regard. Sometimes, it hard to tell the difference.

Come to think about it, most change is difficult and messy. It always has been, and I guess it always will be, difficult. My "model" or "pattern," as far as stories go, is the story of the Exodus when the Jewish people were offered the possibility of change - chance to escape slavery and go to their "promised land." The idea of change is usually much more comfortable than the actual change itself. When the People of God set out from Egypt, they were excited and full of hope about the new future that they could see in their minds' eye.

It did not take long for the pain of change to set in. That pain produced a lot of grumbling, complaining and angry accusations as people began to long for the "good old days" of the past. With selective memory and a desire to escape the pain involved in change, they wanted to "go back." Moses had to keep prodding them to "keep going forward," to "keep their eye on the prize" and never look back.

A few years ago, in serious need of reform, our Church faced a similar opportunity for change. Vatican Council II came along and invited us to enter a process of transformation. I like to compare it to a hatching egg. We woke up one day and noticed that there were fine cracks developing all over the egg. Since then, we have some people running around with tape and ladders insisting that we have to keep it from cracking and "falling part." At the same time, we have some people running around yelling, "stand back, it's hatching, something new is coming out!" I know one thing for sure! The very worst thing you can do when an egg shell is hatching is to try to tape it back together. You will certainly kill the new life that is coming out of it! All the pain, struggle and noise of the post-Vatican II church is not a sign that we are dying. It's a sign that we are giving birth to new life.

The same thing is happening in our country. The "times they are a-changin'." The country is in crisis on many fronts. Part of our country is trying to tape it all back together, trying to recover some by-gone days of our 1950s past. Another part of the country, who suffered and were marginalized during those by-gone days, is yelling "stand back and watch it hatch," we are giving birth to a new America.

The church cannot go back to the stuffy clerical culture of a previous era when the only real players were ordained men. Trying to tape that hatching egg back together is a certain recipe for killing the dynamism that is at the very heart of a living Church.

The country cannot go back to a racist and sexist culture of a previous era when the only players were old white men. Trying to tape this hatching egg back together simply will not work. The hatching process has begun. Women *will* be heard. Women *will* be leaders. Women *will* be actively involved. Black and brown people *will* be heard. Black and brown people *will* be leaders. Black and brown people *will* be actively involved.

We are all uncomfortable during these changing times, but what we do with our discomfort is of extreme importance. There is an old Japanese curse that says, "May you live in interesting times!" During these "interesting times" we have a choice. We can (a) join those who are panicking and trying to "go back to Egypt," trying to tape the cracking egg back together and trying to get the "toothpaste back in the tube." We can "(b) join those who are part of coaching the delivery process along as we wait for a "new Church" and a "new America" come to life.

Misplaced Anger

*Good sense makes one slow to anger, and it is
his glory to overlook an offense.*
Proverbs 19:11

Due to the stresses and losses during the present caronavirus pandemic, many people are experiencing sadness, fear, anxiety and loneliness. As a result many people are feeling angry about their many losses related to jobs, finances, normalcy, routines, cherished activities, the health of self or loved ones, or the ability to see friends and family and they are are engaging in a well-known defense mechanism by transferring that anger to the wrong target. Research suggests that after a loss, disbelief and yearning for former days often occur first, then anger follows.

A common way people protect themselves from unpleasant feelings such as anger is by engaging in defense mechanisms. Displacement is a defense mechanism in which people transfer emotions from the original source to another person or situation. Because defense mechanisms are subconscious, people don't often realize they're taking anger from one situation and blasting it onto another.

Here are some examples. A person who is angry because they lost their parent may take their anger out on the hospice nurse who took care of her at the end of her life. A man who is mad at his co-worker for putting him down in a meeting, might unload his anger on a waitress over a small mistake on his lunch order at a restaurant.

During the coronavirus pandemic, we can be mindful that, along with the shock/disbelief and yearning for the way things were, we are all likely to carry a fair degree of anger, and at times it may be unloaded inappropriately onto people or situations with a little extra intensity.

Because many of us are at home all the time, we need to be especially wary of taking out anger on family members, since those are likely the ones we see the most. We can gain awareness of when we may be "displacing anger," such as snapping at a child for being too noisy while on the phone or yelling loudly at a spouse for not taking the garbage out.

Extreme examples of displacement may be responsible for some of the surges in domestic violence due to the coronavirus pandemic stay-at-home suggestions and orders began.

Once you understand your anger and where you tend to put it, you can make a conscious effort to deal with those feelings in a healthier manner, such as talking with an honest confident or therapist. Going for a long walk to calm down or working out in your home gym might also do the trick.

It's also important to understand when you may be the target of displaced anger, so that you don't take it to heart when a conflict may be about someone else's displaced grief, not you personally.

It's Really About Arrogance

When it comes to trying to understand the present social unrest and the dramatic upheavals in our world, I try to find the common denominator. It occurred to me the other day, that the common denominator underneath so many of our social problems today is plain old arrogance. Arrogance is an attitude of superiority manifested in an overbearing manner or in presumptuous claims or assumptions.

When it comes to our present policing problem, it's not about all policemen. Most policemen are probably hard-working and ethical. It's about the arrogance of a few policemen which has led some of them to be able to literally "get away with murder" in the past. Get rid of arrogance and you will probably solve the policing problem pretty quickly.

When it comes to racial tension, it's not about a difference in skin color. Racism at it's core is about arrogance, an arrogance that believes that white people are inherently more intelligent, more honest and more capable than people of color. Get rid of arrogance and you will probably solve many of the racial tension problems pretty quickly.

When it comes to women's role in society, it's not about sexual difference. Sexism is about arrogance, an arrogance that believes that females are inferior to men in intelligence, ability and emotions. Get rid of arrogance and you will solve many of the problems around the unequal treatment of women.

When it comes to the sexual abuse crisis, it's not about the fact that it exists in the priesthood just as it does in the culture at large. The problem is the arrogance of some churchmen who turned their heads and covered it up to protect their reputations and the institutions they supervise rather than the children and families they are called to serve. Get rid of the arrogance and you will solve much of the present sexual abuse crisis.

When it comes to corporate greed, it's not about the failure of a free enterprise system, it's about the arrogance of some business leaders who deliberately put profits ahead of the health and welfare of the community at large, like knowingly selling asbestos-laced baby power that causes cancer. Get rid of the arrogance and you could probably strengthen the free enterprise system.

Arrogance has at its root a fixation on "me" instead of "we." Arrogance is a failure to consider the fact that we, as human beings, live in community and, as members of that community, we are responsible to and for each other. United we stand. Divided we fall.

WHAT DOES "NORMAL" FEEL LIKE?

The old things have passed away;
behold, new things have come.
II Corinthians 5:17

Many of us might remember the old TV commercial from the 1980s that asked "Is it real or is it Memorex?" The brand of audio recording tapes known as Memorex claimed to offer such an authentic capture, representation, and playback experience that the listener would not be able to tell if they were listening to the actual conversation or performance or it was simply being played back for them on audio tape.

During this pandemic, I find myself wondering whether this "new normal" is actually real or whether I am in a dream from which I can't seem to wake up. It's only been been a little over six months, but I find myself stopping and trying to remember what "normal" felt like.

If I let myself think about it, I can remember other events that are similar when things have radically changed in such a short time leaving people confused about what's real and what isn't.

I still remember sitting on the deck of my nieces's house after we had just buried her husband. She said something I keep coming back to from time to time. "I knew who I was yesterday, but I don't know who I am today!" Her mind had not caught up to the reality that she was in the same house as she was in yesterday, but she was no longer a "wife," but a "widow." It happened so quickly that he was struggling with what was real and what wasn't.

I remember going into the house after my last parent died. What used to be "home" for me was all of a sudden just a "house." It happened so quickly that I was struggling with what was real and what wasn't.

Many soldiers come home seriously wounded after a war, many people come home after a cancer diagnosis, many workers have come home after being told that their jobs have been eliminated and find themselves struggling with what is real and what isn't.

I remember the days after my retirement became a fact. I knew I had been a very active priest for forty-five years, but as I let go of that identity I struggled with what was real and what wasn't.

We are entering a period of grieving. We are struggling with what's real and what isn't. As much as I yearn for "the way things were" and wish that "things would get back to normal," I know in my heart of hearts that we are already in a "new reality" and, no matter how I miss it, there is no way to "go back" really. A stark choice awaits me sooner or later. "Will you choose to stay stuck with your mind in the past and your body in the present or will you reinvent yourself and find a way to adjust and be happy in this "new reality."

We need relief from this nightmare. We need a new hope, a new beginning and a fresh start.

The Freedom to Choose Our Attitude

Metenoiete!
Change the way you think about things!
Jesus

I can't emphasize enough how important the two quotes above have been in my life.

I was raised to believe that life is something that happens to you and all you can do is accept it. In other words, I was taught to be a victim of the things that were happening around me.

Later, I came to believe that working for structural changes would result in making me happy. In other words, if I could get enough other people to change, I would end up happy.

One event in particular caused me to understand the real secret of life and that is to change myself from the inside out. A changed mind was the secret to happiness.

All through seminary, I was told that if you "messed up" they would send you to Somerset. Somerset was as far from Louisville you could get in the diocese in those days.

By the time I was ordained, I had my heart set on an urban assignment or maybe a small city assignment.

When the priest personnel board called to give me my assignment, I was told that I was being sent to Somerset! I was distraught.

Instead of accepting it as inevitable, something that just happened to me, I fought with the personnel board to change its mind. When I failed, I presumed that I was doomed to ten years of unhappiness.

Half way down there, I had a conversion experience. I decided to change my mind. I decided to take back my power and decided that I was going to like it. I decided that it was going to be the best assignment ever! Since I did not get what I wanted, I decided to want what I got. I chose my reaction rather than allowing my reaction make me a victim.

It worked! It turned out to be a great assignment. It opened many doors that led me to places and opportunities I had never imagined for myself. Changing my own mind saved my life! It had to be a moment of pure grace! Grace, of course, is God's gratuitous help, but it requires that we respond positively to that invitation to trust that God has a wonderful gift for you, life to the full! That lesson, changing my mind to change my experience, I have been able to apply many times in the last fifty years of priestly ministry. It has given me power so many times when I didn't think I had any.

We need not be total victims of this pandemic. We can choose how we want to respond to it. We can see only disasters or we can change our minds and see the opportunities even in this situation. This can be a time laced with fear, anger and foolish behavior or it can be a time laced with faith, trust and heroism. We can choose how we want this time to be for us. Yes, we have the freedom to choose our response to this pandemic and thereby choose our experience of it.

> *You have power over your mind – not outside events. Realize this, and you will find strength.*
> Marcus Aurelius

> *Everything can be taken from a man but one thing; the last of the human freedoms - to choose one's attitude in any given set of circumstances, to choose one's own way.*
> Viktor Frankl

www.ingramcontent.com/pod-product-compliance
Lightning Source LLC
Chambersburg PA
CBHW060802050426
42449CB00008B/1489